Rohr — books Buddhist

What Is the Bible?

Also by Rob Bell

How to Be Here

The Zimzum of Love with Kristen Bell

What We Talk About When We Talk About God

Love Wins

Drops Like Stars

Jesus Wants to Save Christians

Sex God

Velvet Elvis

What Is the Bible?

How an Ancient Library
of Poems, Letters, and
Stories Can Transform
the Way You Think and
Feel About Everything

Rob Bell

HarperOne
An Imprint of HarperCollins*Publishers*

HarperCollins books may be purchased for educational, business, or sales promotional use. For information, please email the Special Markets Department at SPsales@harpercollins.com.

FIRST EDITION

Designed by SBI Book Arts, LLC

Library of Congress Cataloging-in-Publication Data

Names: Bell, Rob, 1970- author.
Title: What is the Bible? : how an ancient library of poems, letters, and stories can transform the way you think and feel about everything / Rob Bell.
Description: FIRST EDITION. | San Francisco : HarperOne, 2017.
Identifiers: LCCN 2017018943 | ISBN 9780062194268 (hardcover)
Subjects: LCSH: Bible--Miscellanea. | Bible--Influence.
Classification: LCC BS538 .B45 2017 | DDC 220.6/1--dc23 LC record available at https://lccn.loc.gov/2017018943

18 19 20 21   LSC/H   10

. . . try to love the questions themselves, like locked rooms and like books that are written in a very foreign tongue. Do not now seek the answers, which cannot be given you because you would not be able to live them. And the point is, to live everything. Live the questions now. Perhaps you will then gradually, without noticing it, live along some distant day into the answer.

—RAINER MARIA RILKE

Contents

Part 3

Where That Something Takes Us

Part 4

The Questions That Always Come Up

Part 5
Endnotes

Introduction:
Twenty-Five Years In

To begin with, a bit about where this book comes from.

When I was in my early twenties, I gave my first sermon. I was hooked. I decided right then and there that I was going to give my life to reclaiming the art of the sermon.

I loved giving sermons.
I still do.
More than ever.

And sermons, I understood at that point, are something you give from the Bible. So I went to seminary, and I studied Greek and Hebrew (the two languages the Bible was originally written in), and I studied history and hermeneutics and exegesis and form and textual criticism—all so I could give better sermons.

Eventually I got a job in a church, and I started giving sermons weekly. And then one day something happened that changed everything.

I had just given a sermon, and I was standing around afterward talking to people when a man named Richard walked up to me and said,

You missed it.

What? I asked him. *What did I miss?*

He then proceeded to rattle off a seemingly endless list of things that were happening in the story from the Bible that I had just given a sermon about. Background and hints and meaning and innuendo and humor and tension and history. The more he went on, the more I realized how right he was: I had missed it.

And then he said,

You know, Jesus was Jewish.

What? Jesus was Jewish? I said. I imagine you're laughing at this point because that's so obvious, and yes, I did know that Jesus was Jewish. But not like Richard knew it. Something about that one obvious line set off an explosion within me.

Richard went on to say that Jesus lived in a first-century Jewish world of politics and economics and common stories and inside jokes, and the more you knew about that world, the more he and his message would come to life. Richard began dropping by my office with photocopied articles by people I'd never heard of explaining *mikvah*s and taxation rates and *ketubah*s and who Shammai was and who Hillel was and why that matters. Richard introduced me to friends of his who invited me to eat with them while they would discuss and debate and laugh and riff on the Bible for the sheer joy of it. And they knew their stuff. It was staggering. I could barely keep up. They would point out insightful political commentary or subversive poetry or discrepancies in the text that were actually on purpose because the writer was doing something really clever just below the surface. They'd take a verse or story I'd heard people talk about, and they'd start discussing it and turning it on its head and pointing out all the depth and surprise and power I hadn't noticed—it was like music they were dancing to.

This is in the Bible? I found myself continually asking. *How did I miss this?* It was like the Bible went from black and white to color, from two dimensions to three, or nine.

Gradually what I was learning began to make its way into my sermons and, more significantly, into my life.

And once you see, you can't unsee.
And once you taste, you can't untaste.

People started coming up to me after my sermons, sometimes visibly upset, asking,
How come I've never heard any of this?! This makes so much more sense! This is so much more dangerous and interesting and provocative and timely and progressive and poetic and convicting and funny . . .

Over time I began to realize that what was happening wasn't just that I was learning new things *about* the Bible but that I was reading the Bible in a different way. A way that I hadn't been exposed to. Until now. And now there was no going back.

Which is why I've written this book: I want to help you read the Bible in a better way because lots of people don't know how to read it. And so they either ignore it, or they read it badly and cause all kinds of harm.

Some people see the Bible as an outdated book of primitive, barbaric fairy tales that we have moved beyond. And so they ignore it, missing all of the progressive and enlightened ideas that first entered human history through the writers of the Bible—ideas and ideals we still fall far short of, ideas and ideals that are still way ahead of our present consciousness and practice.

And then there are the folks who talk about how important and central and inspired the Bible is but then butcher it with their stilted literalism and stifling interpretations, assuming that it says one thing and if you just get that one thing, then you've read it well.

But you, I want you to read the Bible in a whole new way.

––––––––––

A few thoughts before we get rolling here.

First, the Bible isn't a Christian book. I say that because many people have come to understand the Bible as a book for a certain group of people to claim and own and then help them divide themselves from everyone else. But the Bible is a book about what it means to be human. And we are all, before anything else, human.

So if you're reading this preface wondering if this is another one of those religious books that's going to try to sign you up and convert you at the end, or it's going to have all kinds of insider language for those in the know, this isn't that book. **This is a book about a library of books dealing with loss and anger and transcendence and worry and empire and money and fear and stress and joy and doubt and grace and healing, and who doesn't want to talk about those?**

Second, you don't have to believe in God to read the Bible. In fact, as you'll see in these passages, the Bible is filled with people wrestling and struggling and doubting and shouting and arguing with this idea that there even is a god, let alone some sort of divine being who is on our side. If you have a hard time swallowing the god talk you've heard over the years, great—this book is for you, because these are exactly the kinds of things the writers of the Bible are dealing with in their writings.

Third, this book is all over the place. Seriously, we're going to jump from topic to topic and story to story and theme to theme, moving from poetry to history to parable to questions and rants. I did this on purpose.

There is an arc, a trajectory to this book. I am trying to take you somewhere specific—but with countless twists and turns. I've arranged this book this way because this is how the Bible is. Yes, it does have an intentional arrangement to it, but there are so many moments when you find yourself thinking, *Where did that come from?*

I've been reading and studying and exploring and rereading and rethinking and giving sermons from the Bible for twenty-five years, and I find it more compelling and mysterious and interesting and dangerous and convicting and helpful and strange and personal and inspiring and divine and enjoyable than ever.

So you can relax—there's a good chance you're going to enjoy this. And you may even find yourself thinking,
How did I miss this?

Part 1

There's Something More Going On Here

1

Moses and His Moisture

In the book of Deuteronomy chapter 34, we read that Moses

was a hundred and twenty years old when he died,
yet his eyes were not weak nor his strength gone.

A fairly straightforward verse, correct? Moses was old . . . and then he died.

What else is there to say? Actually, quite a bit. Read the last half of that sentence again:

yet his eyes were not weak nor his strength gone.

Notice anything unusual? How about that phrase *nor his strength gone?*

Moses has just died, correct?

Dying, as a general rule, is what happens *when your strength has gone.* So why does the writer want us to know that Moses died but his strength *hadn't* gone?

A bit about the word *strength* here. The Hebrew scriptures were originally written in *Hebrew,* and in Hebrew the word translated *strength* here is the word *leho.*

Leho literally means *moisture* or *freshness.*

He died, but his *moisture* hadn't left him?
He passed on but still had his *freshness*?

One translation reads
nor had his natural force abated
while another reads
he still had his vigor
while the JPS Torah Commentary notes that Ibn Ezra understood the verse to mean that Moses

had not become wrinkled.

(Please tell me you're smiling by this point.)

Moisture?
Natural force hadn't abated?
He hadn't become *wrinkled*?

What does the writer want us to know about Moses?

This phrase with the word *leho* here, just to make sure we're all clear, is a euphemism for sexual potency. *That's* what the storyteller here wants us to know about Moses at the time of his death.

That's right, friends, Moses, the great leader of the Hebrews, the liberator who led his people out of slavery, the hero who defied Pharaoh, the one who climbed Mount Sinai to meet with God, the towering figure of the Hebrew scriptures, when he died, *he could still get it up.*

Just so you know.

Which of course raises the question, *Why?*
Why does the writer want the reader to know this?

To answer that question, you have to go back, much earlier in the history of Moses's people, to a man named Abraham. Abraham had many sons, and many sons had Father Abraham, and Moses was one of them.

Abraham, we learn in Genesis, the first book of the Bible, left his father's household and everything familiar and set out on a journey to a new land. People didn't do that at that time in history because they had a cyclical view of history in which everything that has happened will happen again. They believed that you're born into a cycle of events and you'll die somewhere in that same cycle of events as the cycle endlessly repeats itself.

In other words, *there's nothing new.*

What happened to your ancestors will eventually happen to you, and then it will happen to your children as your family goes round and round the cycle.

But then Abraham leaves. He steps out of the cycle. He walks into a new future, one that hasn't happened before. No one had ever done that before because no one had ever conceived of the world and life and the future like that before.

This was a new idea in human history—that you weren't stuck, that you didn't have to repeat everything that had already happened.

But we're just getting started, because to understand the significance of that story about Abraham, you need to back up just a bit more to see that the writers of Genesis told that story about Abraham within a larger story.

There's actually a progression of violence in the early chapters of Genesis, a progression that starts with a man named Cain killing his brother Abel, and then it continues to escalate as all of humanity spirals downward into greater and greater conflict and destruction. By the end of chapter 11—the chapter before we meet Abraham—people are setting up empires to oppress the masses, entire systems perpetuating injustice.

How much worse can it get?

That's the question hanging in the air when the storyteller introduces us to this man Abraham who decides to leave and start something new. He's leaving his home, but he's also leaving an entire way of life.

The storyteller wants you the reader to know that Abraham has a destiny to fulfill in which he becomes the father of a new kind of people to usher in a new era for humanity—one based in love, not violence. As Abraham is told in chapter 12, *all peoples on earth will be blessed through you.*

This was a new idea. They won't conquer other people but bless them?

How do you form a new kind of people that will take the world in a new direction?

You have kids.
And how do you have kids?
You have sex.

And sex involves—that's right—*moisture* and *freshness*.

So when the writer tells you that Moses wasn't wrinkled and his strength hadn't abated and he still had his force, the writer is telling you that Moses was still able to participate in the creation of this new kind of tribe that would take the world in a new direction, away from all that violence and destruction.

Can the world head in a new direction, or are we trapped, doomed to repeat that same old, tired cycle of conflict?

That's the question at the heart of this Abraham-and-Moses story.

But we're just scratching the surface. Because Abraham's tribe eventually found themselves in slavery in Egypt, owned by the ruler of Egypt, Pharaoh. And that's where we meet Moses, who rises up in defiance of Pharaoh and eventually leads the Hebrews out of slavery and into the wilderness, reminding them over and over again of their destiny to be a new kind of people for the world.

Why is this a big deal?
Because if you're a slave, you have one burning question: Will we always be slaves?

Or to put it another way: Will Pharaoh always have the power?

Or to put it another way: Whose side are the gods on—ours or Pharaoh's?

Or to put it another way: Are the deepest forces of life for us or against us?

Or to put it another way: Are we here to suffer, or are we here to do something else, something bigger and better?

Or to put it another way: Does oppression or liberation have the last word? Does injustice or freedom win in the end?

So when Moses led his people out of Egypt, this wasn't just the liberation of a specific tribe—it was the answer to a question people have been asking for thousands of years: **Are our lives set in stone and unable to change, or can we be set free from whatever it is that enslaves us?**

But it wasn't just an answer to a question. This story about Moses and the Exodus was also a warning to anyone who has ever bullied another person, anyone who has ever held their boot on the neck of someone they were dominating, anyone who has ever used their power and strength to dehumanize and exploit the weakness of another:

Your days in power are numbered because the deepest forces of the universe are on the side of the oppressed, the underdog, and the powerless.

For this Hebrew tribe, then, passing this liberating and intoxicating idea along to the next generation was really, really important. That's how you change the world, by entering into your own liberation and then passing that freedom and joy and liberation along to your kids.

And how do you get kids?
You have sex.
And how do you have sex?
Well, as we all know, that involves *moisture* and *freshness*.

You with me here?
Do you see what we just did?

We started with a few obscure English words in the thirty-fourth
chapter of the fifth book of the Bible about a man named Moses.
But then we dipped just a bit below the surface, and in no time we
found a subtle, slightly crude, quite funny, sly, unexpected sexual
euphemism that took us earlier in the story that then circled back
to another story a bit later, and in no time we were dealing with
violence and hope and despair and slavery and oppression and
empires and imagination and human consciousness and the birth
of new ideas no one had ever had before, and you were reading
along thinking about *them* back *then* but when we talked about
whether or not things can change or are they set in stone and
there's nothing you can do about it, you realized

you've had that question before about your own life, right?

So it started with an affirmation of Moses's organ potency, but a
page or two later, we were talking about the despair we all flirt with
from time to time, weren't we?

We started with a line about *his life,* which led us to a line about
their life, which led us to *your life* and *my life,* which led us from the
past to the present to the future to *all of life.*

All that, from reading one line in . . .

the Bible.

———————

Why bother with such a strange, old book?
Because it's a book about *them, then,* that somehow speaks to you
and me, *here and now,* and it can change the way you think and feel
about everything.

But isn't it actually a library of books written across a number of years by people who didn't know each other with agendas and opinions and limited perspectives?
Yes, of course it is. And it's even stranger than that, which we'll get into.

But doesn't it promote violence and all sorts of primitive and barbaric behavior that we've left behind?
No, and I want you to see where that view comes from and why it's so misguided.

But you have to admit that there is a lot of violence in the Bible—like the violence you skipped over just now in that retelling of the Exodus story—and a lot of it is done in the name of God or because the person believed God told them to do it.
Absolutely. There are a lot of those stories in the Bible, and we're going to explore a number of them, because there's more going on there than most people realize.

But it seems like a lot of the people who talk the most about how important and central and necessary the Bible is seem to skip over and gloss and censor the most dangerous and interesting parts about sex and politics and power and the poor.
Yes, so true! This is a dangerous, subversive, explicit, foul, honest, strange, contradictory, paradoxical, ruthlessly hopeful book that makes a number of rather stunning claims about pretty much everything. (Do you like that phrase *ruthlessly hopeful*? I'm quite keen on it.)

But isn't the Bible ultimately about Jesus and how there's a narrow way and a few people will find it and everyone else is going to burn in hell?
No, it's not. It's bigger and more expansive and inclusive and embracing and enlightened than that because the Jesus story is bigger and more expansive and inclusive and challenging and dangerous and enlightened than that.

But isn't it, honestly, quite boring?
If you're bored reading the Bible, then you aren't *reading* the Bible.

Well, then, how do you read the Bible?
That's what this book is about. Because it's easy to read the Bible and miss an entire world of weirdness and joy and hope and innuendo and implication just below the surface.

This book is about that world.
Let's start, then, in the beginning.

2

Somebody Wrote Something Down

In the beginning,

someone wrote something down.

That's how we got the Bible.
Some people wrote some things down.

Obvious, right?
And true.
And absolutely important that we start there.

The Bible did not drop out of the sky; it was written by people.

Many of the stories in the Bible began as oral traditions, handed down from generation to generation until someone collected them, edited them, and actually wrote them down, sometimes hundreds of years later. That's years and years of people sitting around fires and walking along hot dusty roads and gathering together in tents and homes and courtyards to hear and discuss and debate and adapt and change these stories, poems, letters, and accounts.

The people who wrote these books had lots of material to choose from.
There were countless stories floating around, tons of accounts being handed down, massive amounts of material to include. Or not include.

In the Old Testament book of 1 Kings, the author writes in chapter 11,

As for the other events of Solomon's reign—all he did and the wisdom he displayed—are they not written in the book of the annals of Solomon?

Well, yes, I guess they are—it's just that we have no idea what the author is referring to! Interesting, the assumption on the author's part that not only do we know this but also that we have access to these annals. Which we don't.

We see something similar in the Gospel of John, where it's written,

Jesus performed many other signs in the presence of his disciples, which are not recorded in this book.

And then the book ends with this line:

Jesus did many other things as well. If every one of them were written down, I suppose that even the whole world would not have room for the books that would be written.

It's as if the writer, just to wrap things up, adds, *Oh yeah, I left a ton of stuff out.*

The authors of the books of the Bible, then, weren't just writing— they were selecting and editing and choosing and making decisions about what material and content furthered their purposes in writing and what didn't.

The writer of the Gospel of Luke:
I too decided to write an orderly account for you . . .

From the book of Esther:
This is what happened . . .

Toward the end of the Gospel of John:
These are written that you may believe . . .

There were points these writers wanted to make, things they wanted their readers to see, insights they wanted to share, stories they wanted to tell.

What these writers ultimately created was a library. The Bible is a library of books, written by forty or so authors over roughly fifteen hundred years on three continents. This library is vast and diverse and covers a massive amount of ground. At various moments over the past several thousand years, people made decisions about what books became part of their Bible and what books were left out. People wrote the books that became the Bible and then other people decided that those books would or would not be included in the Bible. These people had meetings and discussions and developed criteria and had more meetings and discussions, and eventually they made decisions. Decisions about what the Bible even is.

It's important to point out that these writers—and the people who decided whether or not to include their writings in the Bible—were real people living in real places at real times. Their purposes in writing, then, were shaped by their times and places and contexts and psyches and personal histories and economies and politics and religion and technology and countless other factors.

What does it tell us about the world Abraham lived in that when he's told to offer his son as a sacrifice, he doesn't ask for any instructions on how to do it? He sets out to do it as if it's a natural thing for a god to ask.

The David-and-Goliath story starts with technology—the Philistines had a new kind of metal that the Israelites didn't. The story is undergirded by that primal fear that comes when your neighbor has weapons that you don't have. Like spears. Or guns. Or bombs.

The Roman Empire had a particular line from their military propaganda that began, *There is no other name under heaven given to humankind by which we must be saved.* So when the apostle Peter used this phrase, *there is no other name under heaven,* he's referring to something his readers would have understood.

Real people,
writing in real places,
at real times,
choosing to include some material,
choosing to leave out other material.

And it turns out that what they wrote about was love and fear and debt and duty and doubt and anger and skepticism and hate and technology and shame and hope and betrayal—the very struggles and issues we're still talking about thousands of years later. And that's why it's so important to not read it like it dropped out of the sky. Because in doing so, you miss the solidarity that comes from realizing that this is a profoundly human book.

Now, let's look at a few of the stories these real people living in real places at real times told. We'll start with a story about Jesus writing on the ground because when you're reading the Bible, it's important to remember that **there's usually something else going on.**

3

Stoners and Swingers

In the Gospel of John, there's a story about a woman who gets caught having sex with a man who isn't her husband. A group of concerned religious leaders bring her—and not the dude!—to Jesus and quote the Torah (the first five books of the Bible, also called the Law and also referred to as the Books of Moses) about how she should be stoned for what she (they?) had done.

(The throwing-rocks-at-someone-until-they-die kind of stoned, just to be clear.)

They're trying to trap Jesus by asking if she should be killed ACCORDING TO THE LAW. (That just feels like it should be CAPS LOCKED, doesn't it?) Jesus, however, won't have any of it. He bends down and writes on the ground. He then says,

Let any one of you who is without sin be the first to throw a stone at her.

He writes some more on the ground, the men start to leave until it's just Jesus and the woman, he asks her if anyone condemns her, she says no, and he tells her that he doesn't either and she should leave her life of sin.

End of story.
But beginning of questions . . .

What was he writing on the ground?
And why did whatever he was writing on the ground and what he said
cause the religious leaders to walk away?
And why do the older men walk away first?
Why does John include those details?

———————

This story about the woman and the leaders who want to stone
her is found at the beginning of chapter 8 in the Gospel of John.
If you back up to the previous chapter, chapter 7, you read that it
was the time of the Festival of Tabernacles.

The Festival of Tabernacles was one of the seven major feasts
on the Hebrew calendar. (They're listed in Leviticus chapter 23.)
There were spring feasts and fall feasts, organized around the
agricultural cycles of planting and harvesting. (Feasts were
common in the ancient world in agricultural societies—people
set aside particular times to thank the gods for the latest harvest
and then ask the gods for continued abundance for their crops
and harvests.)

The spring feasts began with Passover, then
Unleavened Bread, then
Firstfruits, then
Pentecost.

The fall feasts began with the
Festival of Trumpets, then
the Day of Atonement, and then
the Festival of Tabernacles.

The Festival of Tabernacles, then, was the last of the fall feasts, and the last feast of the year. As the last of the fall feasts, it was the feast before the winter, when hopefully rains would come and water the crops so they'd grow so that in the spring you'd have food to harvest. If the rains didn't come during the winter, you might not have food and you'd starve.

Thousands of pilgrims in the first century would pour into Jerusalem for the eight days of feasting, staying in makeshift shelters (the Hebrew word is *sukkots*) that reminded them of how their God had cared for their people many years earlier when they had journeyed in the wilderness (that story is told in the book of Exodus).

You can see how a story about how their God had cared for them and provided food would have had particular resonance as they faced a coming winter and the pressing question of whether or not the rains would come and bring them a spring harvest. During the eight days, there were sacrifices and prayers and singing and rituals, oriented around asking God to bring the winter rains so they'd have food in the spring. The religious leaders would teach during these eight days about the significance of water—water as rain, water as divine provision, water and thirst, thirst as a metaphor for spiritual longing. Lots of teaching about water. The eight days all built up to the last day, when the high priest would take a pitcher of water and a pitcher of wine and pour them together over the altar while the crowd chanted,

Hosannah! Hosannah!

Hosannah means *God save us,* as in, *God, please bring us winter rains to save us from drought and famine.* (Later *Hosannah* began to have political connotations, as in *God, save us from the Romans who have invaded our land!*)

With that in mind, notice this line from chapter 7:

On the last and greatest day of the festival, Jesus stood and said in a loud voice . . .

Why is he speaking in a loud voice? Because it's the last day and the crowd would have been chanting loudly. He wants to be heard over the noise of the gathered throng.
And what does he say in his outside voice?

Let anyone who is thirsty come to me and drink.

He chooses this moment, a moment when people were focused on their very real physical needs for water, and calls them to their spiritual thirst, thirst he insists he can do something about. (Is this why earlier in the chapter, he tells his brothers to go to the festival and he stays back, telling them the time isn't right? He's waiting for the last day to make his speech with the ritual of the priest pouring the wine and water and the crowd chanting about their need for a savior as a backdrop. The theatrics alone are fantastic.)

Thousands of people in Jerusalem, feasting and drinking and celebrating and chanting and praying and living in makeshift shelters on the side of the hill in Jerusalem. Basically, religious camping. With a lot of wine involved.

And what often happens when lots of people drink and camp together?

Of course, they end up in each other's tents. And arms.

Can you see how two people might end up in the wrong tent—regretting decisions they made the night before? It's not surprising, then, that the next morning, the teachers of the law and the

Pharisees drag into the temple courts a woman they'd caught with a man who wasn't her husband.

They bring the woman to Jesus because they want to trap him. And so they challenge him with a passage from the law:

Our scriptures say this woman should be killed. What do you say?

Jesus isn't fazed at all by the trap. He bends down and writes on the ground.

And what does he write?

Well, what have the Pharisees and teachers of the law been doing these past eight days?
They've been at the feast.
And what have they been doing at the feast?
They've been teaching.
And what have they been teaching?
They've been teaching about the spiritual significance of water.
And what passages from the Hebrew scriptures have they been teaching on?
Interesting you ask. One of the passages that was taught at the Festival of Tabernacles is from the prophet Jeremiah. The passage is about dust, which is what you have if you don't have water. Here are a few lines:

LORD, *you are the hope of Israel;*
all who forsake you will be put to shame.
Those who turn away from you will be written in the dust . . .

What was the last line again?
Those who turn away from you will be written in the dust . . .

And what did Jesus do?

He bends down and writes *in the dust*. He takes one of the passages they all would have been familiar with, and he enacts it, all without saying a word. They've rejected him, but instead of saying it, he alludes through his actions to a verse they were just teaching, essentially implying that they—the concerned religious leaders—are the ones who have turned away, not the woman.

So what does Jesus write on the ground?
Their names?

You can read this story lots of ways. One way is to see it as a wonderful lesson about how we should all be less judgmental. You know, don't throw stones at people when they screw up because we all screw up from time to time and it's important not to condemn but give people grace because you'd want them to give you grace.

Great.
That's one way to read it.
And we could use more grace and less stone throwing, for sure.

So why the detail about Jesus bending down and writing in the dust?

The storyteller wants you to see that Jesus is confronting an entire entrenched power structure. These spiritual leaders were part of a temple institution that ruled the Jewish tribe, an institution that controlled politics and religion and economics and cultural life. And this institution had become corrupt in Jesus's day. Which is why he confronts them.

And what happens when people confront power structures? What happens when people call out the powers that be when those powers have lost the plot?

Often the person gets killed.

This is not just a nice story about how we should be less judgmental—
this is about political and social resistance to anything that robs
people of their dignity and honor. This is about the courage and
tenacity of this rabbi to stand up and say, "You're in the wrong."
This is a story about Jesus writing on the ground, but it's also a hint
of what's to come. This man is going to get killed.

———————

Did you see what just happened there? We started with a story
that didn't make a lot of sense—Jesus bending down and writing
on the ground and then the teachers walking away. But then we
flew a bit higher and read it in the larger context of what was
happening leading up to that moment, and it quickly started to
go somewhere.

Which leads us to a question:
Who paid Jesus's bills?

(You didn't see that coming, did you? Stay with me, because we're
headed somewhere.)

4

Who Paid Jesus's Bills?

After this, Jesus traveled about from one town and village to another, proclaiming the good news of the kingdom of God. The Twelve were with him, and also some women who had been cured of evil spirits and diseases: Mary (called Magdalene) from whom seven demons had come out; Joanna the wife of Chuza, the manager of Herod's household; Susanna; and many others. These women were helping to support them out of their own means.

—Luke 8

There is so much here, where do we start?

First, Jesus rolled deep.

The literal Greek word here is *posse*. (I couldn't resist.)
As Jesus went from town to town, he was accompanied by a large group of people, both men and women. The disciples were referred to as the twelve. (Get it? There were twelve tribes of Israel, and Jesus is calling Israel back to her roots and mission to be a tribe

that blesses the world, and so he starts by surrounding himself with . . . twelve.) And then a group of women . . .

These women helped pay the bills.
When the check for the meal came to the table for this large group, it was the women who took care of it. (For the record, do you see how crazy it is when religions and faith communities and churches don't allow women to do certain things like *lead* or *teach* or *preach* or *be elders* or *priests*? This movement started with women not only being fully empowered participants but also bankrolling the work. How insane is it when a religious institution has a list of what women can and can't do?)

These women had fascinating stories.
Like Mary Magdalene, who had previously been possessed by seven demons. (Someone counted.) Can you imagine her perspective on things? You can feel Luke's agenda by including a line like that, can't you? He wants you to see what Jesus was about, what he's doing, the kind of people he attracted—the kind of people his message is for.

And then there's Joanna.
Ah yes, Joanna.
Who is Joanna again?
Oh yes, the wife of Chuza.
And who is Chuza?
The manager of Herod's household!

Now *that* is a bomb, dropped right there in the middle of the paragraph.
Why?

A little background: Herod the Great was the king of Israel who died around the year 4. He was a towering figure who dominated the sociopolitical landscape for forty years, building massive palaces and theaters and fortresses, and killing lots of people, including his wife and some of his sons. (He's the one who ordered the execution of those children when Jesus was born.) When he died, Rome decided to divide his kingdom among his sons. Philip got the east, Herod Antipas got Galilee, and Archelaus got Judea, which included Jerusalem. Archelaus quickly made a mess of things and was ultimately replaced by a *Roman* governor named . . . Pilate. (Yes, *that* Pilate.) Philip faded quickly, and Herod Antipas was given Galilee, where Jesus was born and raised.

So when Jesus came on the scene, Herod Antipas was the ruler of Galilee. And Herod Antipas was a very, very rich man. He owned lots of land and had palaces and guards and servants and a massive household, the biggest in the country.

And who managed this king's household?
Chuza.

So Chuza would have been responsible for a massive amount of wealth, which would have brought him a massive amount of wealth. He shares this wealth with his wife, who is traveling with an itinerant rabbi, paying the bills.

Let's pause for a moment and let that sink in: Joanna would have been the elite. Her husband is the president's chief of staff. That's lavish banquets that go on for hours with singers and dancers. That's various homes scattered around the country. That's the best clothes, the best art, the best furniture . . .

That's a life she apparently doesn't find that interesting because she's sharing a room at the Motel 6 in Cana with Mary Who Used to Have Seven Demons. She's sitting around the dinner table with small-town fishermen who are probably in their late teens, early twenties.

She's meeting lepers. She's hearing Jesus give sermons to thousands of people who have come to hear him because they're hoping for free food because they're really hungry.

Now, one more detail. Notice this verse from Luke 13:

At this time some Pharisees came to Jesus and said to him, "Leave this place and go somewhere else. Herod wants to kill you."

Herod wants to kill you.
Of course he does.
Herod rules a kingdom.
And it's absolutely crucial for him that his kingdom remain the only kingdom. But Jesus is going from village to village announcing the arrival of *another* kingdom, the kingdom of God. A kingdom that isn't built around the rich oppressing the poor and the powerful using their military might to keep the weak in submission. It's a kingdom built on compassion and nonviolence and love and solidarity with those who suffer. It's a totally different kind of kingdom.

For Herod, any other kingdom than his kingdom is a threat, and so he wants Jesus dead.

How does Jesus respond to the Pharisees telling him that the most powerful man in the nation is trying to kill him?

Wait—before I tell you what Jesus says, let me give you a bit of background. In ancient Jewish culture, if you were to talk about how great and significant a man was, you would describe him as a *lion*. And if a man was a liar, a fake, a phony, an imposter—we would say a *poser*—you'd call him a *fox*.

So how does Jesus respond when he's told the king wants him dead?

Go tell that fox, "I will keep on driving out demons and healing people today and tomorrow, and on the third day I will reach my goal."

Jesus calls Herod a fox, the biggest slam you could say in that world at that time.

Side note: The symbol of the Romans, who ruled over Herod—and pretty much everybody—was an eagle. And Jesus referred to the Herodians as foxes. So when a man comes to Jesus and wants to become his disciple, Jesus says to him,

Foxes have dens and birds have nests, but the Son of Man has no place to lay his head.

What's Jesus saying here? He's telling the man that his movement isn't about the accumulation of wealth and possessions; it isn't about comfort. Jesus wants the man to know that the kingdom he's announcing isn't like the kingdoms of the Romans or the Herodians.

Now, let's connect all the dots:
Herod wants to kill Jesus because Jesus is proclaiming a kingdom other than Herod's, and that makes Jesus a political threat. But Jesus is able to travel around announcing this subversive message of a different kingdom than Herod's because there is a group of women who travel with Jesus and pay his bills, including a woman named Joanna who has lots of money because her husband is a household manager who gets paid by . . .
Herod.

Herod, in other words, ends up indirectly funding the very resistance movement he's trying to stamp out.

Fascinating, isn't it? That's just a few words in a paragraph in the eighth chapter of one of the Gospel accounts about Jesus's life.

It never ends when you're reading the Bible—you dive in and discover there's a whole world of depth and intrigue and innuendo and story just below the surface. There's always something more going on.

Now, let's fly much closer to the ground. I want to show you how focusing in on just one word in a passage can open up all kinds of new understanding and questions.

5

Anakephalaiossathai

Here's a line from a letter in the New Testament to the Ephesians, written by a man named Paul:

[God] made known to us the mystery of [God's] will according to [God's] good pleasure, which [God] purposed in Christ, to be put into effect when the times reach their fulfillment—to bring unity to all things in heaven and on earth under Christ.

Wait, what?
Bring unity to all things?
All things?

First, a little Greek for those of you keeping score at home.

The phrase *all things* is the word *pas* in Greek, and it translates literally . . . *all things.* (I'm guessing you thought it was going to be something subtle or profound; instead, it's exactly what it appears to be.)

A little recap: According to the writer Paul in this passage, God is doing something through Christ—something involving all things—because it brings God pleasure.

God is a pleasure seeker.
That's what all this is according to—
God's pleasure.

(By the way, when you hear the word *God,* do you immediately
think of *pleasure?* Because that's the engine of this idea here, the
thing Paul is trying to communicate. That God does what God
does for pleasure. Interesting, isn't it, how often there's a world of
meaning in just a passing phrase?)

God enjoys this, whatever it is.

Now, on to the whatever.

The phrase used to describe what God is up to in Christ is
translated here as
to bring unity.
In other translations it's
to sum up
or
to gather up
or
to recapitulate
or
to bring to a head.

The word in Greek is *anakephalaiossathai.*

Let's pause for a moment to appreciate the sheer volume of this
word. If you use this word, you are not messing around. This is the
only place it occurs in the Bible, and you can crush your friends in
Scrabble with it.

Ana means *again,*

Kephale means *head,*
so to *anakephalaiossathai* is to *bring things together under one head.*

(The word was also used in the ancient world in math, describing what happens when you sum up several numbers.)

Sometimes this word is translated *recapitulate.* Another word for *recapitulate* is *retell.* There's a story that's been told a certain way, from a certain perspective, through a certain lens—**but then you retell it,** you recapitulate it, you tell it a different way.

When you retell a story, **you don't remove the nasty bits or the unfortunate events**—you include them. But in retelling things, they appear in a new light. They are what they are, and yet when they're retold, they take on new meaning and weight and perspective.

Remember when you went camping and it rained the whole time and you were soaking wet and then the car got a flat tire and those raccoons got into your food? (Insert a similar story here.) When you tell that story years later at a dinner party, you tell it with a smile on your face with great flourish until everyone around the table is laughing.

It's a great story about *the worst camping trip ever.* Were you laughing at the time your tent ripped and filled with water? Were you smiling when you realized you had no dry clothes left? Were you enjoying that walk to the convenience store in the downpour while you were doing it?

No.
It was miserable.

And yet, when you retell the story, you include all those details because in your retelling, they get transformed.

In fact, you accentuate the nasty bits. It wasn't just a sprinkle; it was a massive downpour involving cats and dogs. Your little sister didn't just get a stomachache from the Little Debbie cakes she got at the gas station that she ate for breakfast, lunch, and dinner; you tell us how she *heaved chunks all night long.*

What were once the worst parts of the story, in your retelling, become the best bits.

Now, back to the verse. According to Paul,

God is retelling . . . everything.

The world is fractured, broken; parts are lying scattered all over the place—and it brings God pleasure to bring it all back together in unity. In Christ.

All of it?
All of history?
All of everything every human has ever done?
Why does Paul use this intentionally expansive word *pas?* Why does he include heaven and earth?
Why didn't he put some boundaries on it?
Why didn't he say *religious things* . . . or *Jewish things* . . . or *redeemed things* . . . or *good things that deserve it?*
Why is it so blatantly inclusive?
Why is he so clear and insistent that nothing is left out of this

*anakephalaiossathai-*ing

that God is up to in the world that brings God so much pleasure?

With those questions in mind, notice what Peter says in Acts chapter 3:

. . . until the time comes for God to restore everything.

And what Paul writes in Colossians chapter 1:

God was pleased . . .
(there's that *pleasure* word again)
. . . and through [Jesus] to reconcile to [God] all things . . .
(there's that *pas* word again)
. . . whether things on earth or things in heaven, by making peace through his blood, shed on the cross.

And here's Jesus in Matthew chapter 19:

Truly I tell you, at the renewal of all things . . .

Retelling?
Restoring?
Reconciling?
Renewing?

What is this?
What are they talking about?
And why do they all use this all things *phrase?*
Why do they leave it so purposely vast and inclusive?

Restoring, reconciling, renewing, *anakephalaiossathai*-ing—they're consistent and persistent in their claims that what God is up to in the world involves putting everything back together as it should be.

Your broken heart?
All things.

Poverty?
All things.

Abuse?
All things.

Racism?
All things.

Fractured relationships?
All things.

All things.
All things.
All things.
All things.
All things.

According to Paul, this is what brings God pleasure.
This is what God is up to in the world.
This is what God is now doing.

Can your story be retold?
Can all of the various things that have happened to you and the
things you have done you'd prefer to never think about again
and the embarrassing parts and the painful parts—can all of it
be retold in such a way that the worst parts become the most
powerful, poignant parts?

And if that is possible for your story, is it possible for the history
of the world? Can everything eventually be retold in such a way
that the worst parts—wars and disease and oppression and on and
on—are included and somehow brought to a unity?

We find this verse in a letter, so it's somebody writing to someone
else. They're telling them what they think and believe. It's a claim,
a statement, an announcement—but you can also read it as a

question, can't you? Like we just did—we turned it into a question, a massive question about what we believe is actually happening in human history.

And implied in the question is another question: *Do you believe this is happening?*

And in that question is another question: *What would it look like to live like this is true?*

Which leads us to the question: *Would living like that make your life better?*

——————

Interesting, isn't it? Because if you were stuck in a hotel in Des Moines in February and you took out one of those Gideon Bibles from the drawer in the nightstand and you opened it randomly to the first chapter of the letter to the Ephesians and you read that sentence about

bringing unity to all things,

you'd probably, like me, skip right over it, wondering what the writer was going on about and hoping that the next part was more understandable.

But then you slow down and learn that there's this massive word just below the surface in the original language that's found nowhere else in the Bible, and it's a word that was used in math, and it's actually two words attached to each other, and it has this subtle nuance involving not eliminating the nasty and unfortunate bits but somehow including them and retelling them, and suddenly things are way, way more profound and provocative.

One of the reasons I show you this word is because I often hear people dismiss the Bible as, well, old. Out of date. Just not that interesting or even intelligent.

But in English, we don't even have a word that is the equivalent of this word. What do you do if you're translating the Bible into English from Greek and your language simply doesn't have the capacity to capture the breadth and depth of this concept in one word? What do you do? How do you translate it? What decisions do you make?

There's the world of the author,
and then there's the world of the translator,
and then there's our world,
and in all of these worlds, some words are common and some aren't and some concepts are familiar and some are totally new. Just coming up with a translation of the Bible in a particular language involves making thousands of decisions about what words you're going to use.

Do you see how . . . and I'm searching for just the right word here . . . how *alive* these passages are? They make claims and give hints and lead to possibilities—and in this case all are unleashed through this one very big word.

6

The Importance
of Altitude

When you read the Bible:

You can read a verse and study the individual words.
You can reflect on a sentence.
You can look for insight in the flow of several verses together.
You can study a paragraph or a chapter.

Or you can fly higher, looking at the entire book.

This is what I mean by altitude: You can read the Bible at different heights, from the up-close scrutiny of a single word to the ten-thousand-foot-high view of an entire book or the entire library itself. And when you fly up high, you often see things that you missed when you were flying closer to the ground.

Like in the book of Acts.
How does Acts begin? With Jesus telling his followers that they'll be empowered to take his message to the ends of the earth, beginning with Jerusalem and then Judea and Samaria. (Remember that; it will come into play shortly.) Jesus, who's Jewish, talking to

his mostly Jewish followers, telling them they're going to leave their Jewish homeland and end up in the farthest corners of the earth.

(By the way, by chapter 8, what do we learn? That they're still in Jerusalem! Interesting, isn't it? He tells them they're going to leave the bubble and go far from home spreading his message, but seven chapters later, they're still there in the world they've always known. We then read that a great persecution broke out against them and they were scattered to—wait for it—Judea and Samaria. It takes a little suffering and struggle to get them out of their bubble.)

Now, fast-forward to the end of the book of Acts. The apostle Paul is in *Rome*. Rome, for a first-century Jew, was truly the ends of the earth. He's rented a house, and he's welcoming all who come to see him, telling them about the kingdom of God.

There's an arc, a trajectory, a movement to the book of Acts that you only see if you fly at a higher altitude, reading the book as a continuous narrative. What you see is that this Jesus message can't be contained by any one group or ethnicity or geographical location or religion. This kingdom-of-God message (that's what Jesus talked the most about, and that's what Paul talked the most about) simply cannot be kept in a box of any kind.

It moves from Jerusalem to Rome,
from the known to the unknown,
from the particular to the universal,
from the local to the global,
from one people group to all people.

It begins with a specific group of people from a specific tribe but spreads until it's at the ends of the earth.

It's an expanding reality, breaking through whatever walls are put around it, spreading and growing beyond whatever boundaries

it's given. The very nature of God's redeeming love and the reconciliation of all things can't help but make its way to the ends of
the earth.

Or, the book of Ruth.
A woman named Ruth, whose husband has died, heads to a new
land, and makes a sexually explicit overture to a man named Boaz.
(Her mother-in-law tells her to go in to him at night and *uncover his
feet*. What else do you think that means?) Boaz then makes her his
wife, and they have a kid. (The book of Ruth in two sentences.)

This story appears on first read to be about an obscure family with
a bitter mother-in-law. Until you read the last two verses and you
learn that the baby Ruth has with Boaz is named Obed, his son is
named Jesse, and Jesse is the father of King David.

Why is this a big deal?

Because at the center of the Hebrew scriptures is this man
Abraham and his tribe who wander and suffer and argue and
wrestle with God. Abraham has a calling to be the father of a
new kind of tribe, one that shows the world the redeeming love
of God. (Notice how we keep circling back to this idea?) But right
away (one chapter after we meet him), Abraham and his nephew
Lot part ways. It turns out that he and Lot have gotten so wealthy
that the land literally can't support all their flocks and hired hands.
Too much stuff in too small a space. Their riches bring them to the
conclusion, *Let's part company. If you go to the left, I'll go to the right.*

If the point is to be a new kind of tribe, things start off tragically,
because we're only one chapter into this new story (Genesis 13)
and this new tribe has already split.

Lot goes one way,
Abraham another.

Until the book of Ruth.

Ruth is from Moab, and the Moabites were descendants of Lot. So when Ruth returns to Israel, this story about this obscure family becomes a story about Lot's tribe and Abraham's tribe being reunited. Ruth coming home and marrying Boaz is about Lot coming home. It's about healing the family. It's about bringing together what was separated years earlier.

(In the Hebrew language here, the same word is used for Lot separating and Ruth not separating. The storyteller clearly wants us to know that this story is about a much larger story.)

That's why the story ends with a bit of genealogy: the tribe is united and healed just in time for their great King David to be born. So from Genesis 13 all the way to the book of Ruth, things aren't right. But in the book of Ruth, they're made right.

And then there's the book of Exodus.
How does it begin? With the Hebrews in slavery in a foreign land, owned by Pharaoh, with their God nowhere to be seen. With God *absent*.

And how does it end? With these slaves freed and living in the wilderness, with a tabernacle in their midst with God dwelling in the tabernacle

in the sight of all the Israelites during all their travels.

The story begins in darkness but ends in light,
begins in slavery but ends in freedom,
begins with the absence of God and ends with the presence of God,
begins with God out of sight, ends with God in sight.

And while we're at it, how about the book of Ephesians?
The apostle Paul writes a letter to his friends in the city of Ephesus, and for the first three chapters, he doesn't tell them one thing to do. He simply tells them who they are. He says they're blessed and adopted and redeemed and forgiven and included and marked and sealed and alive and raised up and on and on he goes, announcing who they are and what God has done for them and how Spirit dwells in their midst.

He just keeps telling them who they are and what's been done for them.

And then, in chapter 4, he begins to tell them what it practically looks like for them to live out this new reality in everyday life.

First, he tells them who they are.
Then he tells them what to do.

Why?

Because the Jesus message is first and foremost an announcement of who you are. It's about your identity, about the new word that has been spoken about you, the love that has always been yours.

If you start with instructions and commands, people might be mistaken into thinking that God loves us because of what we do or how religious or moral or good we are. That's not gospel. Gospel is the announcement of who God insists you are. You're a child of God, not because of how great you are but because God has all kinds of kids and you're one of them.

And if you keep telling people who they are, who their best selves are, if you keep reminding them of their true identity, there's a good chance they'll figure out what to do.

Once again, you fly higher and you spot that little shift from the end of chapter 3 to the start of chapter 4, and it opens up the whole letter, revealing all sorts of insight.

And while we're on a roll, how about the Gospel of Matthew?
Jesus is born, and he's taken to Egypt, right? Then he comes back to Israel, and he's baptized and then spends forty days in the wilderness, right?

Wait—the Israelites were in Egypt, right? And then they were brought through water into the wilderness where they spent forty years.

And Matthew's writing to a Jewish audience. And how does he begin? By connecting Jesus with the history of his people. Jesus is retelling the story of Israel.

And then there's the entire story of the Bible.

How does the Bible begin?
In the book of Genesis with people at peace in a garden with a river and a tree.
And how does the Bible end?
With chapters 21 and 22 of the book of Revelation, with people at peace (no more tears), rivers, and a tree (which is for the healing of the nations), in a city.

Because if you have lots of gardens attached together, what do you get?
A city.

If the Bible was a movie,
the opening scene, involving a tree,
and the closing scene, involving a tree,
are very, very similar.

We live between the trees.

That's why the Bible is not a book about going to heaven.
The action is here.
The life is here.
The point is here.
It's a library of books about the healing and restoring and reconciling and renewing of this world.
Our home.
The only home we've ever had.

So when you're reading the Bible, ask yourself: Is there something I'm missing because I need to fly higher?

———————

When you're reading it, you're interacting with things earlier in the story, referencing things that happened in other places in the Bible, customs, cultures, gestures, words, geography—you're reading it in light of all these other things that are going on around it. And over time, a bit like reading Shakespeare, you start to see some of the same patterns and ideas emerge, and you find yourself getting to *whatever is going on here* much faster.

And then other times, you realize quickly that you're missing something, and then you know what you're looking for. Sometimes huge details are left out because the original audience wouldn't have needed those details.
Like if you told me that

Phoebe was driving us to the rummage sale.

I can picture a car and a steering wheel and putting gas in the tank and finding a place to park. There's a ton of images and associations I have with that sentence that you don't need to explain.

But if you told me that

Phoebe barked the quadrant, raising the glass of every dophax there.

I wouldn't have a clue what you were talking about. I would need some explaining.

That's what's happening in the Bible quite regularly—the writer is referring to something that the original readers would have been familiar with, like that story about the smoking firepots.

7

Smoking Firepots

Let's say you're trying to sell your 1984 light-blue Volvo station wagon, and one day the phone rings. It's a man named Roy, and he says he saw your car on Craigslist and he'd like to come see it. You're thrilled, because you've been wanting to sell that car for a while so you can get one of those killer beige PT Cruisers.

You set a time, Roy shows up, he takes a look at the car and asks if he can drive it. You give him the keys, and as he gets behind the wheel, you ask him where his car is because you suddenly realize that he could just drive off with your car. He says he parked it around the corner. Good enough. He drives away, and you sit down on the front porch with a magazine to wait for him.

And wait for him.
And wait for him.
A half hour later he still isn't back.
You assume he's just a thorough guy.
But after an hour something doesn't smell right, and so you walk around the corner to see if his car is there. As you're walking you realize that you have no idea what kind of car you're looking for because you never asked, and so you go back to your porch.

You wait a little more, you take a walk around the block, but at the two-hour mark you're fairly convinced Roy has stolen your car.

So what do you do?
You call the police.
Why?
Because that's what you do when it looks like your car has been stolen.

Let's pause right there: *you call the police.*

Think of how normal, natural, and perfectly reasonable that response is, and yet how totally astonishing it is. You call a phone number and an officer shows up who asks you questions and has you fill out a form, and then they contact other people who broadcast certain details, and within moments a massive network of experts with staggering technology and skill is looking for your car.

Which they find. At the Circle K, three miles from your house. According to the officer, they confronted Roy as he walked out of the store with a bundle of firewood and a Red Bull–scented air freshener.

Now here's the weird part: When they questioned Roy about why he was driving *your* car, he said that you gave him the keys.

That was his answer: *I assumed it was fine because that nice man gave me the keys to his car.*

When the officers tell you this, you're dumbfounded. What?

But he didn't give me the money for the car! you reply.

When the officers explained to Roy that you need to give someone the right amount of money before you drive away in their car,
he replied,

I've never heard of that. What a great idea.

_____

You find this story strange, right?

You find this story strange and fairly incomprehensible because you
have a deeply ingrained sense of how business works: you agree
to terms, you each provide what you've committed to providing
(money, the car, etc.), and if you fail to do your part, there are legal
consequences.

That's why we have contracts, and that's why we have forms we
fill out, and that's why when you buy things with your credit card
you usually sign for it—you are agreeing to uphold your end of the
bargain. This is true for buying houses, trading horses, and grabbing
a bag of Funyuns on your way home from your weekly squash match.

*Two parties agree to a deal: I'll give you twenty-six dollars a year—you
give me twelve issues of* Horse & Hound.

This entire system exists and survives and works a good portion
of the time fairly consistently because it's undergirded by a law-
enforcement-and-justice system that punishes people for not
upholding their end of the deal. If you don't pay for your Funyuns,
the store calls the police on you.

Now, a question: Four thousand years ago in human history, who
did you call when someone didn't uphold their end of the deal?

Which leads to another question: Before there were these massive, complicated systems of law enforcement and insurance and car titles and wire transfers and cashier's checks and 911 numbers and police scanners—before there were elaborate structures for maintaining justice, how did people ever trust each other to uphold their end of the deal?

Which leads to another question: How did business ever get done if there was no one to call?

Now obviously I've simplified things on a number of fronts here, but one answer is this: *covenant*.

In the ancient world, when you entered into a deal with someone, you made a covenant with them, an oath to do your part.

First, you'd get some animals, like a cow or a ram or a goat or a dove.

Second, you'd chop them in half.

Yep, in half.

Third, you'd lay out the halves with space between them, forming an aisle.

Fourth, you'd stand side by side at one end of the aisle made of animal halves and you'd each state what you were going to do to uphold your end of the bargain.

(You: *I will provide one 1984 light-blue Volvo station wagon that makes an ominous rattling noise over 63 miles per hour.*
Roy: *I will pay $2,713 for the privilege of owning such a majestic vehicle.*)

Why all this?
Because of the next part.

Fifth, you'd then walk between the halves of the animals while you said something like this:

May I become like these animals if I fail to uphold my end of the covenant.

Do you see the power of a covenant like this?
Do you see the significance of this sort of ritual?
(Leaving out the violence-to-animals part for now.)
Do you see the point?

In earlier cultures where systems of justice and enforcement were more primitive and in some cases nonexistent, your word was your bond. Rituals like these were like the glue, the bond, the insurance, the way that people trusted each other, the way that society held together.

May I become like these animals if I fail to uphold my end of the covenant.

By the way, this is where the phrase *to cut a deal* comes from.

_____

All of which leads us to Genesis 15, in which we see God making grand promises to Abraham about the tribe that is going to come from his loins (we'll get to the loins part in greater detail later) that will be a new kind of tribe in the world. Abraham is having a hard time believing God wants to use him to do something like this in the world, especially because of this protest:

What can you give me since I remain childless?

(There's a ton of dark humor here: God tells a man he's going to be the father of a nation, and then the man doesn't have any kids for a really, really long time. It's weird, right from the start.)

God then takes Abraham outside, shows him the stars, and tells him,

So shall your offspring be.

In other words, you're going to have lots of kids. Trust me on this.

Which Abraham does. The next verse reads,

Abram believed the LORD, and he credited it to him as righteousness.

Stay with me here, because this is where things start to take off: In the ancient world, the gods were believed to be distant, detached, petulant, waiting for you to offer them sacrifices to appease their wrath and keep them on your side. That's how people saw the gods. Do whatever it takes to keep their favor. Offer whatever you have to, sacrifice what is needed, go to whatever lengths you can to pacify the anger of the gods.

But this story is about a God who spends a lot of time insisting that this God has plans to do something *for Abraham*.

The story is totally upside down. It's so new and fresh, we don't really have categories for how unheard of this sort of thinking would have been for its day.

A God who wants to do *good* for a person? What?

And Abraham, he believes it. He trusts it. This is revolutionary, and we'll come back to it in a minute. But first a bit more narrative:

God then tells him that God's going to give Abraham some land, and he asks,

How can I know that I will gain possession of it?

God responds,

Bring me a heifer, a goat and a ram . . .

You know where this is going, don't you? Because the next verse reads,

Abram brought all these to him, cut them in two and arranged the halves opposite each other . . .

How come God doesn't have to tell Abraham what to do with the animals?

Because Abraham already knows what to do. He and God are entering into a covenant, they're cutting a deal, and so Abraham does what people in his day did in situations like this.

God then tells Abraham all sorts of things that are going to happen to his people, the sun sets, and in the dark,

a smoking firepot with a blazing torch appeared and passed between the pieces.

God then reaffirms his promises to Abraham, and that part of the story ends.
Wait, what? That's the end of that story?
Yep. A smoking firepot passes between the halves of the animals.

What's the deal with the smoking firepot?
It's a sign of the presence of God.

So God passes through the animals alone?
Yes.

But if God and Abraham are making a covenant, why doesn't Abraham also pass through the animals? Wasn't that how you cut a deal—both parties agreed to do their part?
You're right, that's how it worked. But in this story, God is the only one who passes through. The story starts with something familiar that people at that time did—but then takes an unexpected turn.

So what's the point?
In the story, God commits to upholding both ends of the deal. Even if Abraham fails to do his part, this God will be faithful.

Is there something bigger going on here?
Yes. Abraham is being invited to trust God, to believe that God is good and has his best interests in mind and will be faithful to him even if Abraham makes a mess of things.

That answer feels like it's just scratching the surface of what's going on here.
It is. This is a story about a human being having a relationship with a living God. This was a brand-new idea in human history.

But it's not just a relationship—
Exactly. It's about a particular kind of relationship with a particular kind of God, one who is good and kind and generous. One who can be trusted. One who keeps insisting, *Trust me, I got this.*

But isn't the Old Testament God angry and demanding?
Well, yes, there are lots of those sorts of images of God throughout the Bible, and some of them are really, really violent and awful—we'll get to that shortly. But this story here, this story is about grace, trust, love, and hope.

This Abraham-and-the-smoking-firepot story is about a new understanding of God, a god Abraham is learning to trust more and more.

This story is about an evolution in human thinking about the divine.

It's not just about cutting a deal. It's about a growing understanding of what it means to be human.

It's easy to get distracted with the cutting in half of animals—or to simply skip over it because the smoking firepot image isn't one we're familiar with—and miss how this story represents a giant leap forward . . .

8

And the Fat Closed In Over the Sword

And then there's Ehud, who was left-handed.

The story of Ehud and his left-handedness is in the book of Judges, which as a book is a bit like *Game of Thrones* meets *House of Cards*.

In other words, it's a really violent book involving power struggles and assassinations and questions of who will rule and who will be killed, and where is God in any of it?

According to the storyteller, Abraham's tribe, the Israelites, have done

evil in the eyes of the LORD,

and because of this, King Eglon, king of the neighboring nation Moab, becomes their ruler.

(Side note: Notice how the writer uses the name LORD for God here. That's the name that was given to Moses when he asked what God's name is. It's the name that gets used over and over again to refer to the one who rescued them from slavery and brought them out into a whole new life. Again and again they were called to never forget the kindness shown to them by extending that grace and love and generosity to those around them. But they keep forgetting. They lose connection with their roots. They, as the writer wants us to know, *do evil*.)

(Another side note: Notice how politics and power and faith and religion are all tied into one giant hair ball here. They do evil [which the writer doesn't name] and right away there are *political* consequences.)

This goes on for eighteen years until

the Israelites cried out to the LORD

and the LORD

gave them a deliverer.

Wait—they *cried out*?

That's how the Exodus story started. With the Israelites in slavery in Egypt *crying out*. And God heard their cry. And when Cain killed Abel, Abel's blood *cried out* from the ground. And God heard that cry. And when Jesus is walking through a village and people are *crying out* and his disciples tell him to ignore them, he doesn't ignore them—he hears the cry.

Crying out **is a major theme of the Bible.** People crying out in their misery and pain. We'll return to this later, but for now it's really important to see that the storyteller is connecting the Israelites' oppression under King Eglon with their ancestors' slavery in

Egypt. And God, according to the story, always hears the cry of the oppressed.

Which brings us back to Ehud, who God raises up to deliver the Israelites from their oppressor King Eglon. The first thing we're told about Ehud is that he's left-handed. This was unusual, because then, like now, most people were right-handed. Ehud is sent to pay tribute to King Eglon, and he makes a sword, which he straps to his right thigh.

He gives the gift,
leaves,
and then returns,
telling the king he has a secret message for him.
Eglon tells his attendants to leave them alone, Ehud approaches the king, and

as the king rose from his seat, Ehud reached with his left hand, drew the sword from his right thigh and plunged it into the king's belly. Even the handle sank in after the blade, and his bowels discharged. Ehud did not pull the sword out, and the fat closed in over it.

(That's in the Bible. Word for word.)

Ehud then locks the doors behind him and leaves. The servants think the king must be taking a while relieving himself, and then they finally unlock the doors to find

their lord fallen to the floor, dead.

Ehud gets away,
blows a trumpet,
announces that they've been given victory as they slaughter ten thousand Moabites, and then Moab becomes subject to Israel for the next eighty years.

End of story.
Kind of.

Let's go back to that first detail about Ehud, that he's left-handed. There are three mentions of left-handed people in the Bible, and they're all from the tribe of Benjamin.

Which is funny, because the name Benjamin means *son of my right hand*.

So Ehud's left-handed, and we're told he strapped his sword to his right thigh.

Why is this interesting?
Because King Eglon would have had bodyguards who made sure no one brought weapons into the presence of the king. They would have searched people for swords, searching the inside of the left thigh because that's where right-handed people kept their swords. They wouldn't have thought to search the right thigh because people weren't left-handed.

Except Ehud.
It's his oddness that allows him to sneak a sword in to kill the king and liberate his people.

———————

So what do you do with a story like that?

It's so violent.
The whole book of Judges is.
It's blood and chaos all around.
Even the last line of that story—

and the land had peace for eighty years

—is tainted by the fact that it only took murdering a king and ten thousand others to bring that *peace (if that's what you call it).*

So it's a story about Ehud, the clever and crafty hero, who delivers his people from violence. But he does it with more violence.

Which is fascinating because how does the next chapter start?

Again the Israelites did evil in the eyes of the LORD.

And then we're right back into another cycle where the Israelites are brutally oppressed by another foreign king for twenty years until they cry out—

and you know what happens when they cry out, right?

They're delivered. Again.
And on and on it goes.

You can almost feel the writer's fatigue between the lines, can't you? It's as if the storyteller is chronicling all this violence and rescue, showing us how it isn't working.

Nothing ever really gets better.

And yet just below the surface there's this insistence that God is looking out for these people. Rescuing them, hearing their cry, being really, really patient with them.

———————

Which takes us back to the particular story of Ehud. When you read the Bible, one of the things you are paying attention to is the larger patterns, the things that repeat. Because sometimes the bigger point the writer is making isn't just in the story you are reading—it's where that story is and what the writer places around that story and the larger pattern that story is a part of.

There's a point to the book of Judges that you can only get if you read it as a whole.

Yes, it's about a left-handed liberator and a fat king, but it's also about a tribe that has lost its way. It's about the failure of violence to actually solve anything.

The last thing the writer is doing is approving of or encouraging the violence—the writer wants us to see how pointless it is.

So when you're reading the Bible, you're always asking questions. You're asking questions about the details of a particular passage, and then you're asking larger questions about that passage as it relates to everything around it. What comes before it? What comes after it? Is there any action or phrase or idea that I've seen before?

Sometimes the meaning is in the story itself,
other times the meaning is found in how the story sits among a number of other stories,
and sometimes it's the larger pattern that is the point.

Now, let's move from this idea of patterns to a progression that sits just below the surface in a series of Jesus's teachings.

9

The Thing About
Pearls and Pigs

Do not throw your pearls to pigs.

—Matthew 7

Jesus said that.

These words from Jesus are part of a larger section in the beginning of the book of Matthew called the Sermon on the Mount. It's important to understand that this isn't a random collection of interesting bits and sayings—they're actually arranged in a very specific order because there is a progression that reveals itself when you read it as a whole.

In the section before the section about pigs, Jesus teaches about entrusting yourself to God with all the worries and stresses of your life. He insists that God knows what we need before we ever ask for it. This is calm, grounded, centered, nonreactive living in which we trust that no matter how chaotic or uncertain things are, we will be okay. He's teaching us to have a quiet mind, to silence the voices that can run wild in our heads.

Why is this crucial to our thriving? Because it's easy to spend—or more accurately, *waste*—an extraordinary amount of time and energy on things that we can't control.

Worry is lethal to thriving because it's a failure to be fully present. Worrying about something means you're *there,* not *here*—stuck ruminating on the future, not enjoying the present. Jesus teaches us to be fully present in this moment, not missing a thing right here, right now.

These words of Jesus are concrete, practical, brilliant wisdom for how to live in the world with the most joy. And central to this kind of life is Jesus's insistence that God can be trusted. Chapter 6 ends with him saying,

Do not worry. . . . Each day has enough trouble of its own.

And then chapter 7, which begins: *Do not judge.*

How did we get from *worry* to *judging*?

Because *worrying* is about you,
and *judging* is about others, right?

Yes. Exactly. And that's his point.

Notice the progression: from *do not judge,* he then talks about having a plank in your eye and trying to remove a speck from someone else's and then we get to:

Do not give dogs what is sacred; do not throw your pearls to pigs. If you do, they may trample them under their feet, and turn and tear you to pieces.

What? How did we get from worry to judging to specks and planks to dogs and pigs?

Great question.
Now, an answer.

To thrive, we must first commit ourselves to God's loving care. Which will always mean that we surrender our worry and anxiety and drama and stress.

That's how it begins.

You entrust yourself to God.
You turn it over.
You surrender it.

Then there is a second step: you entrust *others* to God.

We entrust others to God because if we don't, we will inevitably deal with our anxiety and worry and fear by trying to control and manipulate them.

And how do we do this?

Sometimes we try to control others through negative things, like judging them and condemning them and disapproving of whatever they do. We pick them apart. We critique them. We try to shame them into doing things our way.

Have you ever seen a parent deal with their anxiety about their kids by endlessly nagging them about everything under the sun?

When your interior life is a mess, when you're racked with worry and guilt and anxiety, you're desperate for a distraction, something to take your thoughts off of the pain and chaos within you. Which often expresses itself in judging and shaming and condemning others.

People with a high need to control others are generally doing it as a way of dealing with the lack of control they're experiencing within themselves.

(Which is why one of the first things you learn in recovery is that you can't control people, places, or things.)

Other times, and here's the unexpected twist, people try to control others not through negative things but through good things. Like giving gifts and excessive praise—all of it an attempt to control.

Have you ever been given something and instead of being filled with gratitude, you had the ominous sense that the gift didn't come from a sincere and pure place, but that the person wanted something from you? Like it was a gift, but there were strings attached?

Or let's take it further: Have you ever had someone try to do something good for you and yet it produced in you a tremendous feeling of anger and resentment? It was confusing, right? Because it was a good thing and yet it produced a violent reaction in you.

Parents, in-laws, spouses, friends, authority figures—various people do these sorts of things all the time. People give good things, but there's something else behind it, something not good, and everything within you wants to tear the gift (and them) to pieces.

This is why Jesus talks about giving dogs something sacred and pigs something valuable like pearls. He's adding another layer to what he's already taught. He's warning us to be very careful about how we relate to others because if we haven't fully entrusted others to God's loving care, we may be giving them good things for bad reasons. We may be forcing things on them they don't want or they aren't ready for, and they may feel pressured or manipulated. And when people feel like that, they usually lash out.

(Is this why so many people who went to religious schools want nothing to do with religion? It was shoved at them with such regularity and pressure that it sucked all the good right out of the experience.)

Jesus teaches us to be ruthless in examining our hearts and our motives and our reasons for doing what we're doing. If we haven't committed ourselves and then those around us to God's loving care, we will inevitably end up trying to control events and people that are fundamentally out of our control.

(This is especially true in family systems in which there is a way things are done. If someone steps out of line, they often receive tremendous judgment and condemnation. And if they continue on their path, what happens next? Usually the system figures out that the judging and shaming isn't working and so it switches to gifts and praise, trying to *win* the person back into the fold. All of it is a failure to entrust others to God, letting them grow and become whoever they're here to be.)

Think about the people who have influenced you the most, the people you most want to be around, the people who have a peace that you want. I imagine they have a non-anxious presence about them, a calm and stillness that comes from making peace with life. And with that comes a particular posture toward others: they love you and give to you but in a way that doesn't feel pressured or clingy. There are no strings attached. They aren't trying to control you or shame you or get you to do anything because they've surrendered their agenda for you, which is the only kind of person who could ever have helped you in the first place. The twist, of course, is that when you entrust others to God, you now actually can help because you don't need anything from them, you aren't working out any unresolved issues or tensions or need to control through them—you give freely with no strings attached.

It's an odd phrase about pigs and dogs, and it's easy to read it and think,

Huh?

Which takes us back to progression.

When you're reading the Bible and come to a *huh?* part, assume that part flows out of the previous part. Assume the writer is making a case for something. Trust that this is going somewhere and that the twists and turns are intentional.

(Like when the apostle Paul in Romans connects suffering with hope. He's doing something very insightful there when he shows how hope is something that is created within you—it's not a fleeting thought or idea, it's a state of being—that is only shaped when you allow the suffering you've been through to work on you and transform you in particular ways.)

If it sounds odd or shocking, it's probably because the writer is trying to jolt you out of your normal way of thinking.

Take the thing you've just read,
and then place it beside the thing after it.
How do they relate?
Why did the writer place
this idea

after
that idea?

Why are those two odd, unexpected images placed side by side?
(Like in 1 Corinthians when Paul keeps contrasting strength and
weakness, or in the book of Proverbs when being simple is the
opposite of being prudent, or in the Gospels when stories about
outcasts and losers are placed beside stories about leaders and rulers.)

Where does the one thing take you,
and then why is the next thing after it?
Why would the writer place them in that order?

And always, always keep in mind:
the weirder, the stranger, the more unexpected—
it's probably intentional.

That's what's so powerful about so much of the Bible. It's about
the disruption that occurs when you're jarred out of your present
mode of thinking and seeing.

It's the moment of upheaval when you realize that the way you're
living or thinking or treating people isn't working. You're the one
throwing pearls to pigs, and it's absurd. And you need to stop.

_____

We've covered a bit of ground so far.

Let's pause for some review.

We started with the very straightforward truth that **the Bible was
written by real people living in real places at real times**.

Fairly obvious.

Then we moved on to see that there's usually **something going on just below the surface of the Bible**.

So you read it carefully.
You pay attention to the weird bits.
You notice the details.
You fly close to the surface—sometimes you fly higher.
Sometimes just one word unlocks something amazing—other times the bang comes when you read it from a much higher altitude.

You never stop asking questions:
Why is that there?
What is that referring to?
Why does Luke mention that women paid Jesus's bills?
Who were those women?
How does that book begin?
How does it end?
Why does the book of Ruth end with a brief genealogy of King David?
You keep asking, hunting, searching, questioning, assuming that there's more going on here.

10

Turning the Gem

Stoners and swingers
and
massive Greek words
and
fat closing in over a sword
and
pearls and pigs—
we're just getting started.

**In the rabbinic tradition, they talk about scripture having
seventy faces.** So when you read it, you keep turning it like a
gem, letting the light refract through the various faces in new and
unexpected ways.

The Rabbi Lawrence Kushner wrote a book called *God Was in This
Place and I, I Did Not Know,* in which each chapter is a different
interpretation *of the same passage in the Bible.*

**You keep turning the gem,
seeing something new each time.**

That's what we've been doing in this book—
we've been turning the gem.

We read it,
and we let it read us.

We dive into *their* story,
discovering *our* story in the process.

I've heard people say that they read it literally. As if that's the best
way to understand the Bible.

It's not.
We read it literately.
We read it according to the kind of literature that it is.
That's how you honor it.
That's how you respect it.
That's how you learn from it.
That's how you enjoy it.

If it's a poem, then you read it as a poem.
If it's a letter, then you read it as a letter.
If it's a story but some of the details seem exaggerated or
extreme—
like when Samson kills exactly one thousand Philistines
or Balaam's donkey starts talking to him
or Elijah is taken up into heaven before their very eyes—
there's a good chance the writer is making a larger point and you
shouldn't get too hung up on those details.
You read it,
and you ask questions of it,
and you study and analyze and reflect and smile and argue and
speculate and discuss.

Other times people want to know the right answer to a passage in the Bible. As if there is a right and a wrong reading of each verse in the Bible. There are, of course, lots of ways to miss the point and truly read it wrongly. But to say that there's a right way may unnecessarily limit your reading of the Bible.

There are lots of right ways to read it.
In fact, right isn't even the best way to think about the Bible.

How about dancing?
You dance with it.
And to dance, you have to hear its music.
And then you move in response to it.

My friend Kent was doing graduate work in Jerusalem with a rabbi who one day gave the class an assignment to go home and read the story of Abraham offering his son Isaac (which is called the Akedah, or the Binding of Isaac) and then think up as many questions as they possibly could about the story.

They returned to class, and the rabbi asked the students to share their questions. They each had a few. After a few students had read theirs, the rabbi launched into a rant about how dumbfounded he was that they had so few. Hadn't they read the story? How could they have read it and come away with so few questions?

You dance with the Bible,
but you also interrogate it.
You challenge it, question it, poke it, probe it.
You let it get under your skin.

We read it, and we let it read us,
and then we turn the gem,

again,
and again,
and again,
seeing something new
over and over and over again . . .

11

Larry in the Airport

Imagine you're sitting in the baggage claim area at the airport, waiting for your uncle Willy and aunt Frieda to arrive from Sarasota, when you notice a man and woman walk up to each other and embrace. You don't think any more about this man and this woman hugging because this happens all the time in the baggage claim area at the airport. People arrive, and they're greeted by their family and friends and lovers, and then they get their luggage and head for the parking lot.

You don't know who this man is or who this woman is or where one of them is coming from or who is visiting who or what has gone on or is going on between them. It's just a man, and a woman, embracing in an airport.

Now imagine what happens when you do know something about them.

Imagine you learn that this man and this woman are actually brother and sister, and she's been working in a hospital in Malawi for the past three years and they just found out that their father has been diagnosed with brain cancer and only has a few days to live and so she has flown home and there is so much she needs to say to him and now her brother has picked her up at the airport and they're headed straight to the hospital where their family will be together for the first time in years and they will say good-bye to their father and they both know as they embrace that it will be unlike anything they have ever experienced.

Or let's say they're husband and wife, and she's had this dream of being a sculptor, doing shows and having her work sold in galleries, but after she went to grad school they started having kids and then he went to grad school and then she needed to get a job just to make ends meet and now they're both working long hours, trying to raise their kids and pay off school loans and the mortgage and now their oldest kid needs braces and their house needs a new roof and her dream is dead. But on her forty-fourth birthday, she woke up with a profound sense of despair, as if life had made decisions for her that left her with the conviction that she hadn't been true to herself. She shared this with her husband who suggested that he get a job in the evenings and weekends at a local sporting goods store his friend owns so that she could cut back on her hours at work and then they could clear out a space in their basement for a studio for her to start sculpting again. And now it's been three years and she's just returning from a trip to New York where she sold her first two pieces and signed a deal with a gallery, and they did it together and they're exhausted but they're alive in ways they never were before and there's a sense of shared sacrifice, like they banded together to make this happen and there is so much joy between them and he's thrilled for a number of reasons, among them he doesn't ever have to answer another question about golf clubs.

Or imagine that this man and this woman are friends, they've known each other for fifteen years, they went to the same college and at various times they've dated each other's friends but five years ago they moved to different sides of the country. And then, totally unexpectedly, a year ago they began writing letters to each

other, actual paper-and-pen letters, and through these letters
a genuine love has started to grow. They've both been burned
in past relationships—she was engaged but her fiancé called off
the wedding two weeks before the date, and he discovered that
his girlfriend of four years had been seeing his roommate behind
his back for two of those years—and so they decided that they
wouldn't see each other and they would just write for a year and
if, at the end of the year, they were still writing then they would see
each other in person. This has happened—the letters have brought
them together in extraordinary ways as their love has been
building and building as they've shared more and more of their
lives with each other. And now the year is up, and she has come
to visit him. And he has a diamond ring in his pocket. Which she
doesn't know about.

Now, let's rewind.

You're there in the baggage claim—only now you know all of this
history and background and context, and then you see her walking
down the hall toward him.

The scene is instantly electric for you, right?

You watch with different eyes.
You're fully engaged,
filled with anticipation.

Why? Because now you are aware. Previously you were cut off
from the depth and separated from the stories of these people.
But now you see and know and feel a number of things that you
didn't previously. Your awareness has changed, which is, of course,
everything from your perspective.

Now let's say your friend Larry is with you, but Larry has been in
the bathroom this whole time. Larry appears just as the woman

is approaching the man and starts going on about how he can't stand those new hand dryers where you stick your hands in and then wait for the air to turn on because they're loud and he doesn't think they're that much more effective and whatever electricity they claim to save cannot make up for the fact that he always ends up having to wipe his wet hands on his pants, which makes it look like he's just had an accident. "What's wrong with paper towels?!" Larry asks—but you motion to him to stop talking because you are intently watching two strangers meet and embrace. You can't take your eyes off them, you are glued to this scene in front of you, and you realize that you are actually fighting back a tear.

Larry watches you dumbfounded.

Larry thinks you're being a bit of a stalker and says, *I don't get it. A woman gets off a plane and embraces the man who's waiting for her—happens hundreds of times a day. It is the baggage claim of the airport, after all. That's what people do here. Am I missing something?*

You have an answer for Larry, right?
You look him in the eyes, and you say _____ .

(What did you say, by the way? Did you bring him up to speed? Did you tell him the story about the letters or the ring or the gallery or the—you filled him in, right? You didn't just leave him hanging there, did you?)

———————

It's a weird story, isn't it?
The point? *There's something more going on there.* And as we've seen in the first part of this book, the more you know about the more going on, the more the Bible begins to open up in unexpected ways.

Now, let's take it further.

Because it isn't just that there's something more going on just below the surface—**it's the nature of that something.**

To get at what that something is, let's start with a story you've probably heard, the one about Noah and the flood.

Part 2

The Nature of That Something

12

Flood

People in the ancient world told stories about floods. The Sumerians told flood stories, the Africans told flood stories, the Babylonians told flood stories—stories about water and its destructive power to wipe out towns, cities, civilizations, and people were fairly common in the ancient world.

There were even stories about people building boats to survive these floods.

In these flood stories, all that water coming to destroy humanity was often believed to be divine judgment for all of the ways people had made a mess of things. The gods are angry, it was believed, and a flood was their way of clearing the deck to start over.

So when we come to a story about a flood in the book of Genesis, chapter 7, it's not that unusual.

For forty days the flood kept coming on the earth.

This flood in Genesis—the one where Noah builds an ark and his family and the animals wait out the storm in the boat—this story is like the other flood stories because this god is like the other gods—fed up with the depravity of humanity, unleashing divine wrath in the form of a flood.

But then this story does something strange. It ends with the divine insistence that *this is never going to happen again.*

God brings a rainbow and then makes a covenant with Noah.

A what?

A covenant. As we saw earlier, a covenant is an agreement, an oath, a relational bond between two beings.

This was not how the other flood stories ended. In those stories, the gods are angry and everybody dies and the gods are satisfied. End of story.

But this God is different. This God commits to living with people in a new way, a way in which life is preserved and respected.

So why was this particular story told?
Why did this story matter?
Why did it endure?

Several reasons.

First, imagine if you had no pictures of earth from outer space, no weather reports, no Google images, no airplanes—imagine if you'd never been more than a few miles from where you were born. And then imagine a flash flood—massive, undulating, swirling, terrifying water—coming at you out of nowhere and wiping your house and crops and animals and family members away.
Imagine what that would do to your psyche.

You would do what we do whenever we suffer—you'd look for causes. And in the ancient world, it was generally agreed upon that the forces that caused this were the gods who had had it up to here with humans and all their backstabbing, depraved ways and had decided to unleash their wrath.

That's how people saw the world.
That's how people explained floods.

But this flood story,
the Noah one in the book of Genesis,
this one is different.

It starts like the others,
with divine judgment and a flood,
but then there's a twist at the end.
Everybody doesn't die like in the other flood stories.
A family is saved.
And then a promise is made to them.
The story heads in a different direction. A very different direction,
a direction involving rainbows and oaths and covenants.

This was not how people talked about the gods.
The gods are pissed off—that's how people understood the gods.

But this story, this story is about a God who wants to *relate—*
A God who wants to *save—*
A God who wants to live in *covenant.*

This story is about a new view of God.

Not a God who wants to wipe people out,
but a God who wants to live in relationship.

So yes, it's a primitive story.

Of course it is.

It's a really, really old story.

It reflects how people saw the world and explained what was happening around them.

But to dismiss this story as ancient and primitive is to miss that at the time this story was first told, it was a mind-blowing new conception of a better, kinder, more peaceful God whose greatest intention for humanity is not violence but peace and love.

It's primitive, but it's also really, really progressive.

One more thought, this one about unicorns.

(How great was that sentence?)

You'll often hear people talk about stories from the Bible, such as this one, with a certain rolling of the eyes, as in, *Can you believe people still believe this stuff?*

Much of this cynicism is due to the way stories like these have been told—often by well-meaning religious people trying to prove that there actually were two animals at a time that went into an ark.

Yes, the boat really was big enough,

or,

Of course God had a plan for where to put the elephant poo.

That sort of thing. What this stilted literalism does, in its efforts to take the story seriously, is often miss the point of the story. This story was a major leap forward in human consciousness, a breakthrough in how people conceived of the divine, a step toward a less violent, more relational understanding of the divine.

It starts like the other flood stories started,
but then it goes somewhere different.
Somewhere new.
Somewhere better.

I know what you're thinking. You're thinking,
The flood story is a progressive story?
It's a story about a new, enlightened view of the divine?
But countless people are killed!
How is that progress?

Great questions.
Questions we'll get to.

But first, let's look at a few other well-known stories from the
Bible, and then we'll connect them all together.

13

Fish

Next, then, a story about a fish. Namely, a man named Jonah getting swallowed by a fish. (The word *whale* is nowhere in the original story.)

To begin with a bit of background, here are some lines from the book of 2 Kings:
*Then Pul king of **Assyria invaded** the land. . . .*
*Tiglath-Pileser king of **Assyria** came . . . and **deported** the people. . . .*
*Shalmaneser king of **Assyria** marched against Samaria and **laid siege** to it.*

Invaded.
Deported.
Laid siege.

Invading is what happens when you raise an army and then march into another country and take it over using force and power and violence.
Deporting is what happens when you capture the inhabitants of said country you've invaded and forcibly remove them from their homes and jobs and towns and land and then take them far away.

Laying siege is what happens when you surround a city with your army and in doing this sever the city from its food and water sources so that so many people are starving and suffering and dying that eventually they give up and surrender.

The Assyrians, in other words, were mean. Nasty, brutish, violent, oppressive—the Assyrians made life miserable for the Israelites. Year after year after year.

It's during this era in history that a story emerged about a man named Jonah. Jonah was an Israelite. And according to this particular story, Jonah's God tells Jonah to take a message *to the great city of Nineveh*.

And Nineveh was in . . . Assyria.

Assyria? Our worst enemy? Those hated infidels who have made life for our people a living hell time and time again? You want me to go into the center of the beast—and do something good for them? Seriously?

Jonah wants nothing of it, and so he heads to the nearest port, jumps on a ship, and sails in the opposite direction.

Of course he does.
You'd get in a boat too.

Often this story is told in such a way that Jonah's disobedience is the point of the first part, along the lines of: *See what happens when you don't do what God tells you to do?*

But how do you imagine the first audiences would have reacted to this story when Jonah won't go to Nineveh? They hated the Assyrians. Of course you don't go to Nineveh. Would they have cheered Jonah on?

So he gets on the boat, a storm comes, there's a discussion among the crew about the cause of the storm, they determine he's the problem, they throw him overboard, he's swallowed by a fish, he prays in the belly of the fish, the fish spits him out.

He then goes to Nineveh, the Ninevites are receptive to his message, and the story ends with Jonah so depressed, he wants to kill himself because of a gourd.

A gourd.
You can't make this up.

There's so much here, where do we start? We'll get to the swallowed-by-a-fish part shortly, but first, we'll start with the sheer strangeness of this story.

You would assume that a story told by Israelites about Assyrians would stick to fairly straightforward categories of good and bad, right and wrong, righteous and evil.

But the Israelite in this story, the one who supposedly follows God, runs in the opposite direction from God. The word that's used is *flee*. Jonah *flees*. He then ends up on a boat full of "pagan/heathen" sailors who *pray*.

And while they're praying for the storm to stop, Jonah doesn't pray at all. Jonah *sleeps*.

The sailors ask all sorts of questions trying to figure out why this storm has come on them, only to discover that Jonah is the problem, something Jonah knew all along.

And then, when Jonah finally does get to Nineveh, after he's resisted God again and again, these horrible, mean, nasty

Assyrians turn out to be open to God's message, really open—so open that the king orders,

Let people and animals be covered with sackcloth.

Sackcloth was what you wore when you were crying out to God, when you were acutely aware of your sins, when you were asking for God's mercy. The king orders everybody to repent and wear sackcloth—including the animals!

(Animals repenting? Wha . . . ? A fairly surreal detail, to say the least. One of the many hints that the author has a larger, *less literal, more significant* point in mind—a point we'll get to shortly.)

(Another point about that point: When you read the Bible, embrace the weird parts. Animals wearing sackcloth is odd. Take note of the strange parts because they're usually there for a reason.)

We're familiar in the modern world with frameworks that see things in dualistic terms: There are the good people, and then there are the bad people, there is the right thing to do, there is the wrong thing to do, there are the people who have it all together, and then there are the people who don't. There are the winners, and there are the losers.

But in this story the categories are all scrambled. The supposedly righteous Israelite is defiant and lazy and generally prickish (is that a word?) while the supposedly evil and wicked heathens are receptive and open to God's message for them.

And then, in the end, after Jonah has had a change of heart and he's seen this massive, miraculous change of heart in the Ninevites right before his eyes, he's so upset by it that he wants to die.

He says to God,

I knew that you are a gracious and compassionate God, slow to anger and abounding in love, a God who relents from sending calamity.

And then he adds,
Now, LORD, take away my life, for it is better for me to die than to live.

What a bizarre story.
A story in which none of the characters do what you'd expect them to do.

Which raises the questions:
So why did this story survive?
Why did people find this story important and worth telling and preserving?
What does it tell us about how they understand who they are and who God is?

Several answers.
First, this story is about a man, but it's also about a nation. Jonah doesn't want to go to Nineveh because the Assyrians had treated the Israelites horribly. The story asks the question:

Can Jonah forgive the Assyrians?
which is really the question:
Can Israel forgive the Assyrians?

Jonah's angry at the end,
angry that God has been so kind to them.

Of course Jonah is angry.

When you haven't forgiven someone who has wronged you and then something good happens to them—when they are blessed or shown mercy or experience favor—it's infuriating.

Which leads us to a larger theme of the Bible: According to the story that's been unfolding up until Jonah gets on a boat, Israel had a calling from early in its history (Genesis 12 to be more precise—notice how we keep coming back to Abraham?) to be a light to the world, to show the world the redeeming love of God.

A calling they haven't lived up to.

There's a question, then, that lurks in the story of Jonah:
Can you forgive your worst enemy and be a channel through which God's redeeming love can flow to them?

Can you move on from the past, or does the past decide the future?

Are our wounds with us forever or can we heal and be set free from them?

It's a question for Jonah
because
it's *the* question for Israel.

This is why the book of Jonah doesn't end with a conclusion or a judgment or details about what Jonah does next.

The book ends with a question, a question God has for Jonah:
Should I not have concern for the great city of Nineveh?

It's a question for the Jonah character in the story, but at a far more significant level, it's a question the author is asking the audience, an audience who we can only assume would have had many, many personal reasons to answer:

No.

Now, on to the swallowed-by-a-fish part of the story.

Jonah gets swallowed by a fish. Jonah then prays in the fish, and then three days later,

the LORD commanded the fish, and it vomited Jonah onto dry land.

That's in Jonah chapter 2.

Now, some instantly respond to a man being swallowed by a fish and living to tell about it with a rolling of the eyes followed quickly by: *Really? Haven't we moved past all that magical/mythical thinking? Haven't we outgrown these fairy tales? Aren't these the exact sort of claims that have turned off so many people from the Bible—let alone God and faith and Jesus and all that?*

Others have a very different response: *If the Bible says a man was swallowed by a fish, then a man was swallowed by a fish! If you deny that this story happened as the author says it happened, then what about all the other stories? If you deny this one, then aren't you denying all the others with miraculous elements in them? And if you deny this one but affirm others, aren't you essentially picking and choosing which ones you want to believe?*

What do I think? **I don't think it matters what you believe about a man being swallowed by a fish.**

If you don't believe it literally happened, that's fine. Lots of people over the years have read this story as a parable about forgiveness. They point to many aspects of the surreal nature of the story as simply great storytelling because the author has a larger point, one about the Israelites and the Assyrians and God's call to be a light to everyone, especially your enemies.

Right on. Well said.

Just one problem. Some deny the swallowed-by-a-fish part, not from a literary perspective but on the basis of *those things just don't happen.*

Which raises a number of questions: What are the criteria for the denial? Do we only affirm things that can be proven in a lab? Do we only believe things we have empirical evidence for? Do we believe or not believe something happened based on . . . whether we believe that things like that happen or not? (That was an awkward sentence. Intentionally.) Can we only affirm things that make sense to us? Are we closed to everything that we can't explain?

If we reject all inexplicable elements of all stories because we have made up our mind ahead of time that such things simply aren't possible, we run the risk of shrinking the world down to what we can comprehend. And what fun is that?

That said, there are others who say, *Of course he was swallowed by a fish, that's what the story says happened!*

Fine.
Just one problem. It's possible to affirm the literal fact of a man being swallowed by a fish, making that the crux of the story in such a way that you defend that, believe that, argue about that—and in spending your energies on the defend-the-fish part miss the point of the story, the point about allowing God's redeeming love to flow through us with such power and grace that we are able to love and bless even our worst enemies. Arguing about how it literally happened can be an easy way to avoid facing the people in your life you need to forgive.

For the people who first heard this story, the story would have had a provocative, unsettling effect. The Assyrians? The Assyrians were like a huge, gaping, open wound for the Israelites. *Bless* the Assyrians?

The story is extremely subversive because it insists that
your enemy may be more open to grace and love than you are.

That's why the book ends not with a conclusion but a question.
A question God has for Jonah—which is the question God has
for Israel—

Should I not have concern for the great city of Nineveh?

This story demands what is called *non-dual awareness*. Many see the
world in dualistic terms, terms in which there are the good people
and the bad people, the sinners and the saints, us and them—a
world in which people stay true to the labels and categories we've
placed them in.

But this story wants none of that. It blasts to pieces our biases
and labels with the declaration that God is on everyone's side,
extending grace and compassion to everyone—especially those we
have most strongly decided are not on God's side.

Religious people have been very good over the years at seeing
themselves as *us* and seeing people who aren't a part of their group
as *them*. But in this story, the dude who sees himself as *us* is furious
because of how chummy *God* and *them* have become. He's so
furious, he'd rather die than live with the tension.

**Which takes us back to the fish: it's easy for the debate about the
fish part to provide a distraction from the tensions of the story
that actually have the capacity and potential to confront us and
disrupt us with the kind of love that can actually transform us into
more mature and courageous people, people who love even our
enemies. (Nod to Jesus there.)**

Now, let's take it further. It's possible in defending the literal
"facts" of the story to be missing the point of the story that can

actually change your heart and in the process can be turning people off from engaging the Bible.

You can argue endlessly about fish, thinking you're defending the truth or pointing out the ridiculous outmoded nature of the man-in-fish miracle, only to discover that everybody in the discussion has conveniently found a way to avoid the very real, personal, convicting questions that story raises about what really lurks deep in our hearts.

———————

See what we did there?
We read this story keeping in mind the people it was first told to and that took us way past ridiculous arguments about fish to something much more profound and personal and pressing about each of us and how important it is to forgive and love our enemies.

Now, one more story, this one about Abraham being told to sacrifice his son, and then we'll start to tie together the big idea that connects the flood, the fish, and the son.

14

Son

Then God said, "Take your son, your only son, whom you love—Isaac—and go to the region of Moriah. Sacrifice him there."

—Genesis 22

What kind of God would ask a man to sacrifice his son?

That's the question about Genesis 22, isn't it?

And to get to the answer, we'll need to first spend some time on the history of religion. Then we'll notice a few details in the story, and then we'll answer the question.

The history of religion, then, in one paragraph: Early humans came to the realization that their survival as a species was dependent on things like food and water. And for food to grow, it needs sun and water in proper proportion. Too much water and things wash away, not enough and plants die. Too much sun and plants wilt, not enough and they die as well. These basic observations brought people to the conclusion that they were dependent on *unseen forces they could not control* for their survival (which was actually a monumental leap at that time). The belief (I use that word intentionally) arose that these *forces* are either on your side or they aren't.

Your crops grow or they don't, you're able to have kids or not, your animals stay healthy or not. And how do you keep these forces on your side?

The next time you have a harvest, you take a portion of that harvest and you offer it on an altar as a sign of your gratitude. Because you need the forces (gods, goddesses, divine beings) on your side. Now imagine what happened when people would offer a sacrifice but then it didn't rain or the sun didn't shine or their animals still got diseases or they were unable to have children— obviously, they concluded, they didn't offer *enough*. And so they offered more. And more and more. Because religion had built into it from the very beginning something called *anxiety*. You never knew where you stood with the gods. The gods are angry, the gods are demanding, and if you don't please them, they will punish you by bringing calamity.

But what if things went well? What if it rained just the right amount and the sun shone just the right amount—what if it appeared that the gods were pleased with you? Well then, you'd need to offer them thanks. But how would you ever know if you'd properly showed them how grateful you were? How would you know you'd offered ENOUGH? If things went well, you never knew if you'd been grateful enough and offered enough, and if things didn't go well clearly you hadn't done . . . enough. *Anxiety either way.* (This is why the book of Leviticus is so revolutionary—we'll get to that later.) Now, stay with me here, because this is where things get dodgy. Whether things went well or not, the answer was always: *Sacrifice more. Give more. Offer more.* Because you never knew where you stood with the gods. And so you'd offer part of your crop. And you'd offer a goat. Maybe a lamb. Maybe a cow. Maybe a few cows. Maybe some birds. The very nature of early religion is that everything escalated because in your anxiety to please the gods, you kept having to offer *more*. And what's the most valuable thing you could offer the gods to show them how serious you were about earning their favor? A child. Of course. Can you see how child sacrifice lurks on the edges of the Old Testament? It's where religion took you. To the place where you'd offer that which was most valuable to you.

Now, to the Abraham story.

When God tells Abraham to offer his son, he isn't shocked.

Early the next morning Abraham got up and loaded his donkey.

Abraham gets right to it. He doesn't argue, he doesn't protest, he doesn't drag his feet. He doesn't even ask for instructions. He clearly knows what to do, and so he does it.

Of course. That's how Abraham understood the world worked. The gods demanded that which was most valuable to you. And if you didn't give it, you'd pay the price. That's how people saw things at that time.

So Abraham sets out and reaches the place on the third day.

For three days he and his son travel, three days in which his son is as good as dead.

When they get to the mountain, what does Abraham say to the servants? (Come on now, you know this!) (Actually, I wouldn't know either if I hadn't read it.)

He says to them,

Stay here with the donkey while I and the boy go over there. We will worship and then we will come back to you.

Wha . . . ? Abraham is going to offer his son, right? That's what the story is about, correct? God telling Abraham to offer his son and so he does it—or at least proves that he would do it—that's the point, isn't it?

But what Abraham says to the servants is that he's going to go offer his son *and then come back with his son.* (All the lights on your dashboard should be blinking by now. There is something else going on in this story. Just below the surface. The story is subverting itself, begging you to see something far more significant going on.)

As they walk up the mountain, Isaac asks Abraham where the sacrifice will come from—this is so morbid, isn't it? As many have understood the story, he's going to his death *because his dad loves God so much.* (Please tell me you find this utterly repulsive. I remember a well-known preacher telling me that when his son was a teenager, he took his son up on a hill and read him this story, and then the preacher told his son that he would always love God more than him. He told me the story like it was an admirable thing he did to teach his son about devotion to God. I wanted to throw up.) But we've already seen Abraham tip his hat that something else is up. So we're not buying that angle.

Abraham's answer? *God . . . will provide.*

Clever. It's a nonanswer answer. Abraham is in on the joke. Or whatever it is you'd call it.

And then Abraham gets ready to offer his son, but he doesn't because God stops him and then *God* offers a ram instead. End of story.

Except that it isn't.
An angel shows up and says that Abraham is going to be
blessed and
through your offspring all nations on earth will be blessed.

**So, back to our original question: What kind of God would ask a
man to sacrifice his son?**

Now, an answer: Not this one.

The other gods may demand your firstborn, but not this God.

So if God doesn't want Abraham to offer his son, why the charade?

Several responses:
First, the drama is the point. Abraham knows what to do when
he's told to offer his son because this is always where religion
heads. So at first, this God appears to be like all the other gods.
The story is like the other stories about gods demanding acts of
devotion and obedience. Gods who are never satisfied. The first
audience for this story would have heard this before—it would have
been familiar.

But then it's not. The story takes a shocking turn that comes
out of nowhere. This God disrupts the familiarity of the story by
interrupting the sacrifice. Picture an early audience gasping. What?
This God *stopped* the sacrifice? The gods don't do that!

Second, the God in this story *provides*. Worship and sacrifice was
about *you* giving to the *gods*. *This* story is about *this God* giving
to *Abraham*. A God who does the giving? A God who does the
providing?

That was a new idea at that time. Mind-blowing. Groundbreaking. A story about a God who doesn't demand anything but instead gives and blesses.

Third, Abraham is told that God is just getting started, and that this God is going to bless Abraham with such love and favor that through Abraham everybody on earth is going to be blessed. This God isn't angry or demanding or unleashing wrath—this God has intentions to bless everybody. **Not just people who love and obey and offer sacrifices to this God. This God intends to bless all people, everywhere.**

And what is required of Abraham? Trust. Faith. Belief. No sacrifice needed, just the belief that this God can be trusted.

Can you see how many new ideas are in this one story? Can you see why people would have found this story compelling? Can you see why people would have felt the need to pass this story along? Can you see why it endured?

Now, let's explore the nature of what's going on just below the surface in these three stories.

15

He Had No Idea What I Was Talking About

Floods,
fish,
and a son.

Those are three of the most famous stories in the Bible. And they're often the stories that people point to when they're insisting that the Bible is a primitive book deeply out of touch with the modern world.

A flood in which God orders the destruction of everybody on earth but one family?
A man being swallowed by a fish and living to tell about it?
A God who commands someone to kill his kid?

Crazy.
Barbaric.
Destructive.
Fairy tales.
Outdated.
The list goes on.

But then we read them, **keeping in mind what the world was like at that time.** And what we saw was that in each of those stories, there was something new happening. Something better. Something pulling people forward.

An understanding of God not based on *destruction* but *relationship*.

Forgiving your enemies so that you wouldn't keep the violence in circulation.

A divine being who wants to bless. And show favor. A divine being who provides.

These ideas were all leaps forward for that day.
Progress.
Enlightenment.
Hope.
The raising of consciousness.

When you read the Bible in its context, you learn that it's a library of radically progressive books, calling humanity forward into a better future.

The point of the Abraham-and-Isaac story isn't that you should sacrifice your kid but that you can leave behind any notion of a god who demands that you sacrifice your kid.

Do you see how huge this is?

Several years ago I had a conversation with a fancy-pants famous pastor (please tell me you're laughing at the description) who has a massive following and had written me a letter because he had concerns about my work. (I learned that *having concerns* is what leader folks say when they're really disturbed.)

We started talking and he started asking questions and quite quickly I noticed that when I would say something good about how I understood God he would immediately say something violent and awful about God.

For example, I might say,

Jesus spoke about the renewal of all things, and I think it's fascinating that he didn't speak of some things, or Christian things, or religious things, but all things,

and then he would counter with,

But God might decide to send everybody to hell to torture them forever,

and then he'd quote a verse from the Bible.

Then I'd say something like

Isn't it interesting how when the apostle Paul wrote about Jesus dying on the cross, he said it's all part of the reconciliation of all things?

and then he'd say something like

But God told them to kill all the women and children in that village in the book of Judges, and sometimes God commands you to do difficult things that you don't understand.

Everything I said, he countered with a verse or story from the Bible about how cruel and punishing God might decide to be—including his continual insistence that God just might decide to send everybody to hell to burn forever because all of humanity deserves it. When I pointed out that if God is like that, able to decide that about all of humanity, then couldn't God possibly decide not to send everybody to burn forever in hell? If God is that random, as this pastor kept insisting, why does it always have to be *horrible* random? Couldn't God go both ways on the random thing? Why not *good* random? Isn't that the God who Jesus talked about? The one who gives people equal pay for working fewer hours and invites the losers to the parties? (Actually, that is Jesus's point! Over and over again, that's his point!)

To which this pastor would inevitably counter with something about how you can't trust those sorts of stories because of . . . and then he'd quote something brutal from the Old Testament.

If you're thinking, *That sounds like it was a fairly awkward conversation,* it was.

We went back and forth like this for a bit until it dawned on me what was going on between us, and I said,

I don't read the Bible like a flat line. I don't see all of the passages in the Bible sitting equally side by side so that you can pick one and then counter it with another and go back and forth endlessly, endlessly leading you to the barbaric and violent and random nature of life— and God. I read it looking for what the story is doing, what's happening within it. What new perspective is emerging? What new idea is being presented? What sense is being heightened? The stories in the Bible—and the Bible itself—have an arc, a trajectory, a movement and momentum like all great stories have. There are earlier parts in the story, and there are later parts in the story. The story is headed somewhere.

He said he had no idea what I was talking about.

Ouch.

So, let's review: **The Bible was written by people.**
People wrote things down over a long period of time.

These things they wrote down, some of which began as oral tradition, gradually took shape as the library we know to be the Bible. Books were left out, writings were edited, things were added, decisions were made about which books belonged, and eventually the library of books we know to be the Bible came to be THE BIBLE.

These things people wrote down reflected the world at their time in their context. These stories they told and the explanations they gave for how and why things happened like they did were filtered through the categories and understandings of the world they lived in.

When you read the Bible, then, **you read it as an unfolding story. You don't edit out the earlier bits or pretend like they're not there; they reflect how people understood things in that time in that place. You read the stories in light of where they're headed.** The earlier bits reflect how people understood things at that point in history, but the stories keep going.

The Bible comes out of actual human history, reflecting the funky, flawed, frustrating world these stories came out of. And right there in the midst of those stories, you often see growth and maturing and expanding perspectives.

Now, let's talk about all that violence in some of those stories.

16

All That Violence

The LORD had said to Abram, "Go . . ."
So Abram went . . .

—Genesis 12

In the ancient Near East, your tribe was your family, your bloodline, your home, your identity—your tribe was everything. And everyone belonged to a tribe.

You worked for the well-being of your tribe, as did everyone else in the tribe. You accumulated possessions, fought battles, made alliances, all in the name of tribal preservation. And if you did something unacceptable, something shameful, it reflected poorly on your tribe.

According to the story in Genesis 12, God calls a man named Abram to be the father—the leader—of a new tribe. (We just keep returning to this, don't we?)

Abram is promised that

all peoples on earth will be blessed through you.

Tribes at that time existed for their own well-being and preservation. (You see the humor in that last sentence, right? Like anything has changed in thousands of years.) But this tribe, the one that Abram would lead, would be different. (An idea that is still ahead of its time.) This tribe would exist to bless all the other tribes.

This was a brand-new idea.

As this tribe of Abram's kids grew, they carried with them this sense of calling, this sense that they were different, that they had a unique role to play in the world.

Tribes had gods and goddesses, forces they followed and worshipped who, they believed, protected and guided them. So when you went into battle against another tribe—usually for land or access to resources or wealth—you were doing battle with them, but at the same time your god was confronting their god. (That's what's going on in the David-and-Goliath story.) And when you won, you wiped them out and took all their stuff. Why? Because what if you left some of the men alive, and then later they banded together—maybe the son of the king you killed was their leader— and they came to get their revenge? You couldn't risk it. Or maybe you killed the men but took the women for yourselves. And the donkeys, and whatever else you wanted. Those were called the spoils of war. There were rules about how this worked, because tribes had been doing it this way for a long time.

Brutal? Yes.
Violent? Yes.
Primitive? Yes.
Barbaric? Yes.

Your tribal identity wasn't just about your bloodline and your gods—it was also about safety. The world was extremely dangerous, and without the protection of a tribe, you could easily find yourself enslaved or worse by another tribe. This was not like picking a political party or religious affiliation in our world—in that world at that time your survival was at stake. When you read those Old Testament stories about So-and-So accumulating so many fighting men and a certain number of swords or horses or camels or making an alliance with King So-and-So, this wasn't a hobby. This was life or death. Kill or be killed. And no matter how many battles you'd fought and won, you were always one battle away from the enemy crushing you and wiping out your entire tribe, or killing some of you and taking the rest back to be assimilated into the conqueror's tribe. (This is why hospitality was so important— when strangers wandered into your camp, you invited them in and cared for them and made sure they were treated well because the slightest snub or inhospitality could set off who knows what kind of intertribal conflict and violence. Which is what is going on in the story about Sodom and Gomorrah . . .)

Imagine what would happen if the tribe next door obtained a new technology, like iron or bronze. It would be terrifying, knowing that if there was battle, you would be outgunned. Your entire way of life would be at stake. (That's the tension between the Philistines and the Israelites during the David-and-Goliath story.)

It's in this world at this time that we read the story of a man called to be the father of a new nation, a new tribe, one that would exist not just for its own self-preservation but also for a much higher purpose—to bless all the other tribes.

This is the story of Abraham's tribe, also called Israel.

Can you see how radical this idea was?

Can you see how this idea would have taken a while to catch on? (And can you see why Jesus keeps reminding his people of their original calling?)

Can you see how difficult it would have been to make this kind of leap in a culture in which tribal affiliation and preservation were the highest values?

Can you see how no matter what you'd been told about who you are and what your calling was, you would still have a filter, a lens, a way that you saw the world?

_____

In light of this,

does it surprise you when someone in the Bible wins a battle and then gives their gods the credit?

That's what people did at that time.

Does it surprise you when after winning, they wiped out the women and children and then said their gods told them to do it?

That's what people did at that time.

Does it surprise you when they won and then let no one escape but put everyone to the sword, and then said they did it with their gods' power?

That's what people did at that time.

Does it surprise you when Lot says,

Don't rape them, have sex with my daughters?

That's what people did in those situations.

Does it surprise you that the view people had of their gods is quite similar to the views their neighbors had of their gods?

That's how people saw the world.

You find these stories violent and repulsive and barbaric

because they are.

If you didn't find them shocking and awful and confusing, something is wrong with you. And people who read these stories and say, *Well, that's just how God is,* have a very, very warped and dangerous view of God.

The violence isn't that surprising; what's surprising is that among all that violence are new ideas about serving and blessing and *nonviolence.*

Here's what I mean:
Do you find it primitive and barbaric to care for widows, orphans, and refugees?
That's commanded in the book of Deuteronomy.
Do you find it cruel and violent to leave a corner of your field unharvested so the poor can have something to eat?
That's commanded in the book of Leviticus.
Do you think people should be set free from slavery?
That's the story of the book of Exodus.
Do you think it's good to love your neighbor?
That's commanded in the book of Leviticus.

What you find in the Bible are stories accurately reflecting the dominant consciousness of the day, and yet right in among and sometimes even within those very same violent stories, you find radically new ideas about freedom, equality, justice, compassion, and love.

New ideas sit side by side with old ideas. Vicious violence is right there next to new understandings of peace and justice. (Kind of like now.)

_____

One more truth about all that violence in the Bible: **you being shocked and repulsed by the violence in those stories may be the writer's intention in telling those stories.**

As we keep coming back to this theme: Somebody somewhere decided to edit and arrange these particular stories in this particular way. There was something they were trying to say by what they included and what they left out.

The Hebrew scriptures (sometimes called the Old Testament) were compiled for the first time in Babylon. Why is this significant? Because Jerusalem was conquered in the 500s (BC) by the Babylonians—the military superpower of their day—and a number of the citizens of Jerusalem were forced into exile, in Babylon. They found themselves miles from home in a foreign land surrounded by people who didn't talk like them or think like them or believe like them.

They found themselves on the receiving end of horrific violence, and it's there that they edit together a series of texts that include . . . horrific violence.

Which is their point.
Those stories containing senseless violence point out how senseless violence is!

It's as if the editors who compiled these stories are just as horrified by all that violence as we are.

These stories end up being a critique of the cycle that is perpetuated whenever someone goes to battle thinking God is on their side.

All of which leads us to another dimension of something more going on here, this one involving
then and *now*.

17

Do What to Our Whats?

(Alternately Titled Bite Down Hard, My Man)

*Abraham was ninety-nine years old
when he was circumcised.*

—Genesis 17

Circumcision? Really? Yes. There's something going on in this Genesis 17 story about God and Abraham that teaches us about how we grow and evolve as humans, something that has tremendous significance for each of us today, especially in reading the Bible.

A bit about circumcision: We've continually seen that the early parts of the Bible are about the formation and identity of a new kind of tribe, a tribe led by Abraham, a tribe with a calling to show the world the redeeming love of God.

And how do you grow a tribe?
There are several ways, the most obvious being: you have kids.

And how do you have kids?
You have sex.

And how does that work?
Excellent question, because the ancient world had a much more limited knowledge of biology than we have. They didn't know what we now know about conception and zygotes and sperm and eggs and all that—what they observed is that a woman didn't get pregnant until she'd been with a man. They concluded then, that the man must be the one who has the life force/seed/magic bullet within him and that when he gives it to the woman, that's when life begins. And for him to give it to her, he passes it through his . . . you're with me here, right?

Every male among you shall be circumcised . . . and it will be the sign of the covenant between me and you.

Circumcision was how these people (okay, men) demonstrated their commitment to being a part of this new tribe and then growing and building this new tribe. A dude, without any drugs or painkillers, would have skin cut off of the most potent/vulnerable point of his body as a way of saying, *I'm in. I believe. I trust. I want to do my part in this new thing God is doing.*

Picture Abraham, ninety-nine years old, biting down on a towel while his neighbor Jeff takes a stone and goes to work . . . (It's not like they had sharp metal knives or ibuprofen or anything like that.)

(And if you're wondering why men would put themselves through such pain, remember that initiation rites usually involve some sort of pain, whether it's a fraternity or a sports team or an intern at a law firm working hundred-hour weeks.)

As the story progresses, we see circumcision becoming more than just a little operation on the man's point (ha-ha) but a whole way of dividing the world, with some people being circumcised and others—*heathens, pagans, you know, everybody who isn't us, etc.*—being referred to as *uncircumcised.* (Remember the shepherd boy David hearing Goliath going on and on and asking the men standing next to him, *Who is this uncircumcised Philistine?*)

Circumcision was a sign of tribal identity, a mark that you were committed to being a new kind of people in the world.

———————

Now, fast-forward a number of years to the New Testament. The apostle Paul—a member of this tribe—is traveling around the ancient world telling people about Jesus. And there is a group of people from his tribe hot on his trail, telling people that if you want to follow Jesus, you have to be circumcised. That's part of the deal, they say—*it's been the sign from the beginning.*

Picture a group of Greeks or Romans who have never heard of Abraham, never read the Torah, never made any commitments to being a new kind of tribe for the world.

But they're compelled by the Jesus message about a new humanity. And now they've just been told that if they're going to follow him, they are going to need to have a little operation. They stand there dumbfounded, saying,

You want us to do what to our whats?

———————

The point is very simple. And yet it's one of the main reasons so many get so tied up in knots reading the Bible.

First, when Abraham is told he's going to be a father for the first time and then he's going to become the leader of an entire nation, he's a ninety-nine-year-old man.

Abraham laughed at this.

God makes people laugh in the Bible. (When you hear the word *God,* is that one of the first things that comes to mind? *Laughing?*)

Tribes need initiations, rites, rituals, ways of determining who's serious and who's not, who's in and who's not, who wants to be a part of the new thing and who doesn't.

And the way these wandering tribesmen thousands of years ago did this was through circumcision. It was a sign, a mark, a tangible demonstration of your identity.

Until it wasn't.

By the time his first followers were spreading Jesus's message, it had become a major source of conflict, with some saying you needed to be circumcised to follow Jesus and others, like Paul, saying you didn't.

This conflict is at the heart of the letter to the Galatians in the New Testament, in which the apostle Paul uncorks an epic rant about how people getting circumcised to follow Jesus *isn't a gospel at all* and anybody preaching a gospel involving circumcision is *cursed* and anybody believing them is *bewitched* and *enslaved*—at one point he writes about these pro-circumcision people,

I wish they would go the whole way and emasculate themselves.

The Greek word here for *emasculate* is *apokopto*. It literally means *to cut off.*

I wish they would cut theirs off.

———————

So how did circumcision, which was central to the story early on, become a problem later?

How did something that was considered good—and commanded by God early in the story—become something Paul calls *enslavement?*

First, Paul doesn't have a problem with circumcision. It's important to point that out. He has a problem with how it's being used. It's a good thing, being used in a bad way.

———————

Second, if you take two bits out of different places in the Bible and hold them up side by side, they may appear to be saying very different things *because they are saying very different things.*

You'll often see this in criticisms of the Bible. People quote a verse from one place and refer to a story from another and then mention a passage from earlier or an idea from later as evidence of how primitive or contradictory it is.

You have to read it differently.

You have to ask where you are in the story. You have to read it not as a flat line, in which you can pick and choose, but as a reflection of how people saw things at different places in the story.

I regularly get questions about the Bible that begin with a line like this,
Why didn't God just . . .

followed by something like this,
. . . send everybody to heaven so they wouldn't have to suffer?
or
. . . skip the sacrificial system because it was pointless?
or
. . . not put that tree in the garden?
or
. . . come up with some way to fix things without Jesus having to die?

Behind these sorts of questions is the belief that the Bible records one version of events that could easily have been changed if God had just decided to act in some other way.

But that's not what we have in the Bible. What we have are poems, letters, and stories written by real people living in real places in real times.

When Paul talks about circumcision, he explains it as something meaningful at that time, something that served its purpose, something that pointed forward to what was coming.

It wasn't wrong; it was *then*.
And *then* is not *now*.

So when people take *then* and try to make it *now*, they're missing the point, working against the fundamental orientation of this library we call the Bible.

(Are there things that were true then that are true now? Of course.)

And this library is about the God who meets us at whatever place we're at and invites us to trust and believe that there's more. That we're just getting started. That we've only just begun.

So why don't we just ignore the earlier bits?
The reason why the earlier bits are so interesting is that they show you what growth and movement look like. Part of the power of reading earlier stories is when you spot the movement, it can better help you spot movement in your life and world now.

When I was starting out as a pastor, I would often hear people say,

We need to get back to how they did it in the early church.

The idea behind this statement was that there is an ideal state or culture or way of doing things that if you could just get back there, then you'd be all set.

But reading the Bible, you learn that it's not about trying to be something you're not—it's about learning to see the movement and motion and possibilities right in the midst of whatever world you find yourself in. We're not living in the first century or the ancient Near East—we're here, now. At this time. In this world.

And so we don't need to replace one culture with another; we open our eyes to the divine invitation right here, right now in this one.

_____

Next, a few stories about Jesus before we ask the question: *How did Jesus read the Bible?*

18

Give It Up for Sidon!

In Genesis 9, a man named Noah plants a vineyard (*after* the boat ride), then he gets drunk, and he ends up naked. His son Ham sees him, tells his brothers, they cover him up, and from there things get ugly. Noah wakes up, realizes what has happened and curses Ham's family, beginning with Ham's son Canaan.

In the ancient world, cursing was a big deal. Especially from your father. Cursing was way more than just words—it was about your father's favor, your father's blessing, your father's validation. To be cursed was devastating—it stayed with you, it haunted you, it hung over your life like a dark cloud.

So Ham's son Canaan was cursed, which meant that Canaan's sons were cursed, beginning with his oldest son, Sidon.

Sidon, it turns out, had a number of sons, so many that Sidon went on to become the father of a nation. A nation that is mentioned again and again in the Bible.

In Judges 10 the Sidonians conquer and oppress the Israelites.

(Interesting to note how it starts with a father cursing his son, but the wound festers to such a degree that a few generations later, the son's nation is oppressing the father's nation. Wounds always linger and spread, don't they?)

(Also interesting to note how if a wound from a father isn't dealt with and eventually healed, it inevitably affects more than just the person who was originally wounded. Why are these two nations at war? Answer: Because a father cursed a son.)

(And while we're at it, this is why the Bible continues to have such resonance: Have you seen any movies recently in which the main character has unresolved issues with his or her father? Of course you have. We're still telling the same stories, still working through the same pain. In thousands of years, things have changed—and yet they haven't.)

More on the Sidonians:

King Solomon marries a number of Sidonian women, who lead him to worship their goddess Ashtoreth. (1 Kings)

Several generations after Solomon, the Israelite king Ahab marries the Sidonian princess Jezebel, who turns out to be trouble. (1 and 2 Kings)

The prophet Isaiah predicts terrible things for the Sidonians, telling them to be silent and ashamed, and that they will find no rest because of all the wrong they've done. (Isaiah 23)

The prophet Jeremiah talks about the coming day when there would be no help for Sidon. (Jeremiah 25, 47)

And Ezekiel, never one to miss a chance to heap judgment on the neighbors, talks about the Sidonians going down with the slain in disgrace . . . lying uncircumcised, bearing their shame. (Ezekiel 27, 28, 32)

The Sidonians, as I'm assuming you're seeing here, are the bad guys in the story. They're the proverbial bad neighbors, the evil empire, the oppressors next door.

_____

Which brings us to Jesus's day.

Generations of animosity against the Sidonians had built up a head of steam in the first century, to the point where many from the Jewish tribe wouldn't dare go to Sidon or even talk to someone from Sidon. This bias went all the way back to the story about Noah, and as we know from our world, when bigotry and hatred have generations to fester, they can become very, very entrenched.

So that was the common belief among Jesus's tribe: We're the faithful, the chosen, the ones God loves.

We're in; enemies like the Sidonians are out.
We're on God's side; they're not.

But then, in the book of Mark chapter 7, Jesus goes to Sidon.

Huh?

And then in Matthew 15 Jesus has conversations with Sidonians in which he's amazed by their faith.

What?

In the Gospel of Luke, people from Sidon come and find Jesus *and he heals them.*

And then in the Gospel of Matthew, Jesus is going through the towns of Israel, and the people from his own tribe are rejecting him and refusing to respond to his miracles, and he announces *that Sidon will be better off on the judgment day than them.*

Why is this interesting?
In Jesus's world, the Sidonians were believed to be cursed, the curse resting on them going all the way back to Noah, many generations earlier.

Jesus couldn't care less.
He simply dismisses the history of his tribe with the Sidonian tribe.
He comes to heal that wound, literally healing actual people from Sidon.
And then, to take it way, way further, he insists that these hated enemy Sidonians are actually in better standing with God than the people who believe they have favored status with God.

According to Jesus,
better to be a Sidonian than a devoted religious person who thinks the Sidonians are cursed.

———————

So what do we learn from the Sidonians?
There's an interesting thing Jesus says after the part about the day of judgment. He says that God has

hidden these things from the wise and learned, and revealed them to little children.

In a highly religious culture like the one Jesus lived in, people held their views and convictions and loyalties with clenched fists. (Uhhhh, kind of like now.) Stories about who had God's favor and who didn't, who was cursed and who wasn't, held tremendous power.

But according to Jesus, God is interested in something else. How open are you to what Spirit is doing in this moment? How receptive is your heart to a fresh word about grace? Are you hungry to learn, to grow, to be transformed? Do you want to see things in a new way?

Because if that's the desire, it doesn't matter where you're from.

Should we kill our enemies?
No, Jesus said to love them.

Should we make judgments about who is in and who is out?
Whenever people did, Jesus quickly and decisively acted to include whoever had been excluded.

What about the curse that was so important to Jesus's tribe for so many years?
He invites his tribe to leave it behind.

He does this often, challenging his tribe to think about things in a new way. Like the story about the good Samaritan.

19

He Can't Even
Say His Name

or

The Reason Why People Miss the Point
of the Good Samaritan Story

Everybody knows the story about the good Samaritan, right? It's about the importance of helping people who are in trouble.

And yes, you *could* make it about that. And that might be helpful. But you'd be missing the point of the story.

Here's why: Jesus tells this story (it's in Luke 10) in response to a question. And the more you understand the question, the more you can see just how brilliant and provocative the story is.

The question is asked by a lawyer, who wants to know: *What must I do to inherit eternal life?*

A couple of truths about this question this lawyer asks:

First, the lawyer is a scripture expert. That's what lawyers were in the first century. So he's asking a question, but he already has an opinion. That's what scripture experts did in the first century: they had discussions about their opinions. This man is not new to the game; he's one of the elite, a long-standing member of the religious establishment. It's important to note that whatever Jesus says, this man will have something to say in response to it.

Second, when the lawyer asks about eternal life, he's not asking about the afterlife. What happens when you die was not something people in Jesus's day talked much about, and it wasn't something Jesus talked about much at all. The focus in the first-century world that Jesus inhabited was this life, this time, here and now. *Not life after death but life before death.* So when you had a chance to interact with a great spiritual teacher or rabbi, that was one of the first questions you would ask them: *How do I have the most/best/fullest life right now?*

Eternal life was that phrase people used to describe a particular divine quality of life, the kind that comes from living in harmony and peace and connection with God.

Jesus, of course, responds like a good Jewish rabbi, asking the man what the Torah teaches. Jesus responds this way because in the first-century Jewish world, the answer to how you have the best, most full and vibrant life was believed to be in the Torah (that's the first five books of the Hebrew scriptures—Genesis, Exodus, etc.). How does it teach you to live?

The lawyer isn't surprised at all by Jesus's question to his question.

Let's pause here and note that Jesus responds to his question with a question. This, once again, was not at all unusual for his day. Jesus is asked lots of questions in the Gospels, and he responds to almost all of them with . . . a question.

The lawyer isn't surprised at Jesus's answer-that's-a-question because life revolved around the Torah and so Jesus's answer-that-is-really-a-question is how he would have expected him to respond. The lawyer then quotes Deuteronomy and Leviticus that loving God and loving your neighbor are the most important things you can do—they're how you enter into this particular kind of life called *eternal life*.

Jesus then says to him, *That's cool.*

Well, not exactly. But pretty close. Jesus responds, *You have answered correctly. . . . Do this and you will live.*

Which is the end of the exchange, right?
What else is there to talk about?

Man asks a question, Jesus asks him a question about his question, he answers the question about his question, Jesus tells him he got it right. Conversation over.

Except it isn't.

(By the way, we aren't even to the good Samaritan part yet and you can already smell something is up, can't you?)

Another parenthesis, just for good times:

(When people say the Bible is boring, they're saying that because they haven't actually read it. Because if you actually read it, and enter into the stories, and the depth and background and context and innuendo and hyperbole, the one thing you will not be is bored.)

The conversation isn't over, because the text reads,

But he wanted to justify himself, so he asked Jesus, "And who is my neighbor?"

Ohhhhhhhhhh. Interesting . . . **the dude had an agenda all along!**
It's a setup. All that question-and-response and love-your-neighbor
blah-blah-blah was all a setup! The lawyer has an issue with Jesus;
he disagrees with Jesus, and his questioning was to get to the point
of conflict. Which has something to do with who your neighbor is.
It's as if he says,

*Yeah, yeah, yeah, we can do Torah all day and agree that loving your
neighbor is how you get eternal life, but we both know that you and I,
Jesus, don't agree on who our neighbor even is.*

At which point Jesus then launches into the story about the good
Samaritan. A certain man was going to Jericho from Jerusalem and
was beaten and left by the side of the road. A priest comes along
and passes by on the other side—

Let's stop there.
That's funny.
The road between those two cities was a trail a few feet wide.
With a wall of rock on one side and a drop-off on the other. **Jesus
is being funny here because there was no other side.**

Then a Levite (a religious leader) comes along and does the
same thing.

A third dude comes along. Let's point out that the logical thing for
Jesus to do in the story here is make the third person who does
stop a . . . lawyer. Then Jesus could have made his point to the
lawyer about how your neighbor is anyone you're passing by who
is in need.

Which is how a lot of people tell this story.
But that completely misses the point.

It isn't a lawyer who comes along, it's a—wait for it—*Samaritan*. And teachers of law and lawyers-the-scripture-experts *hated* Samaritans. This is the last character the lawyer would have expected to enter the story. Samaritans were the pedophiles-who-kick-puppies of the day. This hatred went way back, generations back, and it ran really, really deep. But in this story Jesus tells, the Samaritan *helps* the man.

This story would have been next to impossible for the lawyer to hear. A *good* Samaritan? In our day when people use the phrase *Good Samaritan,* it is said without disgust or irony or most of all *disbelief.* It's not a paradox *now.* It was *then.* A good Samaritan was an impossibility. It didn't exist. Jesus then finishes this story in which a Samaritan is the hero and asks the lawyer,

Which of these three do you think was a neighbor to the man who fell into the hands of robbers?

Boom! Do you see how brilliant and clever and subversive Jesus is here? The whole thing started with the lawyer asking Jesus a loaded question, didn't it? And so what does Jesus do? He tells a story that appears to ramble way off into the deep weeds, then a shocking character enters the story and ends up the hero, and then Jesus turns the table on the lawyer and asks, Who was the neighbor?

The answer is *the Samaritan,* right?
But how does the lawyer answer?

The one who had mercy on him.

You realize what's going on here? The lawyer can't even say the word *Samaritan.* That's how deep his hatred goes. He can't even say the word.

Have you ever noticed how people often refer to the person they used to be married to as their *ex?* How rarely do you hear them actually say the person's name?
Names connect us. Names bond us. Names create intimacy. It feels terrible to forget someone's name, doesn't it?

But this lawyer, he can't even answer Jesus's question by saying the name. He simply replies *the one* . . .

That's your neighbor.
That's who you're called to love.
That's where the eternal life is found.
In showing kindness to the one you hate, the one you despise, the one you wish didn't exist, the one whose name you can't even say.

Now obviously some people we avoid. Some people we have boundaries with. Some people are so toxic and dangerous and hurtful, some people have done so much damage to us that we have to keep our distance. We love them from a distance. That's all part of being healthy. But even then, we forgive so that the hate and bitterness won't eat us alive.

Do you see why I began by talking about the point of the story? You can make it about roadside assistance, which is fine, and maybe even helpful, but Jesus is calling us to something way bigger and higher and deeper and transcendent. Jesus is calling the man to love like God loves. Which means everybody. Even those you hate the most. Even those who are the most difficult to love. Even those you hate so much, you can't even say their name.

20

The Whole Melchizedek Thing and Why You Love It and Know It's True

Let's go back to Abraham—which we keep doing, don't we?

After the battle against King Kedorlaomer, Abraham is traveling through the king's valley when he meets King Melchizedek of Salem, who brings bread and wine and blesses Abraham.

Why is this interesting? Because Melchizedek is described as *priest of God Most High*.

What?

The story starts with Abraham. Everything is falling apart, the violence between two sons has escalated into a whole world at odds with itself, people are trying to build a tower to the heavens to become like gods—it's gotten so out of control that Genesis 12 begins with something new starting, a new tribe, through this particular man, Abraham. A new kind of people to take creation in a new direction.

That's the story we find in the Bible.

But then on his way back from battle, Abraham runs into a man who is a priest of God Most High. And this man *blesses* Abraham.

Wasn't *Abraham* supposed to do the blessing?

And then Abraham *gives him one-tenth of everything.*

Why does Abraham give a tithe to *Melchizedek?*

If this is a story about the new thing God is doing, how come a character shows up who is already in on the new thing God is doing, so much so that he actually blesses Abraham? And then why does Abraham give him a tenth of the spoils?

That's how you treat a *god.* You give them tithes and offerings.

And to further the mystery, we don't get any background on Melchizedek, other than that he's the king of righteousness. (That's what his name means.) Generally, kings are kings of *something.* An area, a landmass, a group of people, a nation, etc. But this king is the king of *righteousness.*

And then he's gone.
He enters the story, and then leaves.

Abraham moves on, Melchizedek goes to who knows where, and we don't hear about him again. The narrator doesn't seem to have any interest in giving us more information. He shows up, he blesses and serves bread and wine, and then the action moves elsewhere.

Until the Psalms. And the book of Hebrews.

Which we'll get to in a minute.

But first, let's circle back to the question of what is called *particularity*. Because for a number of people, their problem with the Bible is what they perceive to be its narrowness. It appears to be about this *one group* of people and not *all* people. It appears to be too *tribal* and not *universal* enough.

Why this one tribe?
Why this one particular group of people?
What about all of the other people and tribes and religions and perspectives? Isn't the Bible too narrow in its insistence that God works through this one story of this one tribe that comes from this one man, Abraham?

Great questions. You should be asking those questions. If you read the Bible and you don't have those questions, you're probably not reading the Bible.

Which is why the Melchizedek story is so compelling.

Within the Bible itself, and especially here in the opening pages, is a clear example of someone knowing God, walking with God, blessing people in the name of God, without having any connection with the particular Abraham story that is unfolding.

You see why this Melchizedek story is so significant, right?

The criticism of the Bible is often from those who see it as limiting the divine presence, prohibiting the possibility that people outside of this one particular story can have a genuine connection with the divine. But if you read the Bible, you quickly discover that this is not the story that it tells.

Melchizedek is a deeply mysterious, open, and welcoming character who appears on the scene, blessing Abraham (who was actually still called Abram at this point) in the name of God.

And how does he bless, besides the prayer he says over Abraham?

He brings bread and wine. Which provides an excellent segue to Jesus.

Melchizedek is mentioned in the Psalms once, and then the only other time he appears in the Bible is in the book of Hebrews, where the writer is trying to explain how Jesus can be understood as a priest, but not the kind of priest that people had any categories for. And how does the writer do this?

By comparing Jesus to *Melchizedek*.

Jesus is said to be a priest
in the order of Melchizedek,
a priest
of God Most High
who is a priest
not on the basis of a regulation as to his ancestry but on the basis of the power of an indestructible life.

Interesting, isn't it? That when the writer tries to search for a way to explain how God works in new and fresh ways through already-existing structures, the image that writer uses is . . . Melchizedek.

So what does all this about Melchizedek have to do with us here and now in the modern world?

Don't be surprised when you meet people who have none of your religious background (and baggage) and yet clearly have a genuine connection with the divine. This is normal, healthy, and *biblical*.

Don't be caught off guard when people show up from outside of whatever system or institution or religion or perspective or doctrine or worldview or culture you've created and they have something profound and good to give to you. This is often how the story goes, isn't it?

Don't let lame critiques of the Bible sidetrack you from actually reading the stories. These are radical, progressive, open, expansive, extraordinary stories about the God who is bigger and broader and beyond any one tribe. These stories are told from the perspective of actual people living in space and time, and they often do reflect the limited perspectives of those times and places. But so do the stories we're telling right now. It's all on a continuum, a trajectory, and if you keep this in mind, reminding yourself that these are human stories before they're anything else, it will free you to not only see our common humanity, but you may even find the divine lurking there in all that bone and dust and spirit and blood.

Jesus said that his *Father is always at his work*. This is an excellent assumption for us to live with as we go about our lives. *The divine is always at work*. So when someone you don't recognize from outside your religion, family, or tribe shows up with bread and wine and maybe even a blessing, it may be the Most High God, giving you what you need, blessing you, reminding you who you are and why you're here.

Now, let's pause and think back through these last three chapters, because there's something going on here between Jesus and the nature of that something that's going on just below the surface when you're reading the Bible.

In the Sidon story, Jesus was interacting with his tradition and how they'd interpreted the story about Noah and Sidon, essentially saying,

I don't see it that way.

Then, in the good Samaritan story, Jesus and the lawyer were discussing just what exactly it looks like to love your neighbor, a command from the book of Leviticus, which is really a question of:

Who is my neighbor?

And we quickly discovered that Jesus and the lawyer had very different answers to that question.

In both cases, we see Jesus doing something with the Bible. Commenting on it, correcting people's views of it. And then in the Melchizedek chapter, we saw how one of the New Testament writers used that story to explain who Jesus is and what he's up to in the world.

All of which raises the question:

How did Jesus read the Bible?

21

So How Did Jesus Read the Bible?

How did Jesus read the Bible?

Three words we'll use to explore this question:
interpretation,
incarnation,
and
invitation.

First, then, *interpretation.*

In Jesus's day, no one had a Bible.

This was roughly 1,500 years before the invention of the printing press, and people didn't own books, let alone Bibles, because books didn't really exist.

What people read—
and only certain people—
were scrolls,
and scrolls were rare.

In a village like the one Jesus would have lived in, there would probably have been just a few sacred scrolls, and those scrolls would have been kept in the local synagogue in a cabinet called an ark. There were scrolls of the prophets' writings (Isaiah, Jeremiah, etc.), the wisdom writings (like the book of Job), the history books (the life of King David, etc.), and then there would have been the Torah scroll (Torah is the name for the first five books of the Bible: Genesis, Exodus, Leviticus, Numbers, Deuteronomy).

Torah means *way* or *teaching* or *law* or *instruction*—and everything in Jesus's first-century Jewish world centered around the Torah.

On the Sabbath day you'd go to the synagogue in your village and the *hazzan* (the worship leader) would take the Torah scroll out of the ark and parade it through the congregation, inviting everyone to dance in honor of the Torah.

The scroll would be opened, and someone would read that day's Torah portion—which was mapped out years in advance—along with readings from the prophets, and then there would have been commentary and discussion about what it means and how you live it.

And everybody joined in.
It was assumed you had an opinion,
and it was assumed that you had questions.
Of course you had questions—
questions were a sign of life,
a sign this mattered to you,
a sign you were engaged with the text.

Think of the images that come to mind when you hear the word *Bible*. For many, their first thought is of someone with their head down, alone, reading a bound book with pages. A book they probably own their own copy of. Or maybe the picture that comes

to mind is of someone behind a podium in a church service or on
cable television reading from the Bible and then telling you what it
says or what you're supposed to do.

Contrast this with the Bible in Jesus's world, which was a scroll that
you saw and heard someone reading
in the center of the room,
in the midst of the community.

And then you all discussed it.
You surrounded the words—
you encircled them literally, physically—
and then you engaged with them.
Together.

It was a communal experience.

Picture all that energy swirling around the room,
picture all those opinions,
picture really wise people saying interesting and profound things,
picture that crazy uncle rambling on and on and making no sense.

And then you'd come back the next week and do it all over again.

The Torah started the discussion.

For many in our world, the Bible ends the discussion. Someone
stands up and reads from the Bible and then tells the gathered
masses what it means and what is right and how it should be
interpreted and then the service is over and everybody leaves.

But in the first-century world of Jesus,
the Torah and the prophets and the wisdom writings were the start
of the discussion.
You read it, together.

And then you interpreted it.
You engaged with it.
You turned the gem.

This wasn't just an intellectual exercise.
This was about life.
How do you live?
What do you do?
How do you act?
How do you treat people?
How do you conduct yourself?

Think whatever you want,
let your mind wander,
but how you act—
that's what matters.

So when people come to Jesus and ask him questions in the New
Testament Gospel accounts, most of the time they're asking him
questions about the Torah and how it should be interpreted.
Which is why almost every time he's asked a question, he responds
with a question:
How do you read it?
or
What do you think it says?
or
How do you interpret it?

Some people interpreted it one way,
and some people interpreted it another way.
The role of the rabbi evolved over the years as powerful,
charismatic rabbis emerged who made all sorts of compelling
interpretations of the Torah that would get handed down through
the generations.

All of it done in a desire to live the fullest life.

There's an ancient commentary about the Torah being like a
blueprint of the universe. For Jesus's tribe, the Bible wasn't just
a helpful religious text—it also revealed the deepest realities of
the universe. There's another commentary about how when God
gave the Torah, not the sound of a bird chirping was heard and
how seventy tongues of fire went out into all the world so that
everybody could hear the Torah. They believed that God gave them
the Torah at Mount Sinai in the wilderness in a marriage ceremony
between the divine and the human.

They saw the Torah, then, as an expression of love.
As the ultimate union between heaven and earth,
between the divine and the human.

Jesus's tribe understood these books as both particular to
their tribe,
written by their people,
and yet worldwide and universal—
the divine words for everybody everywhere, for all of creation.

And it had to be interpreted.
You read it. Your people read it.
And then you made decisions about how to live it out.

You made decisions about what it means to love your neighbor.
You made decisions about how to honor and respect life.
You made decisions about how exactly you keep one day holy.
You made decisions about how to best care for the poor.
And on and on it goes.

You lived with the assumption that there was always something
new to learn, always something new to discuss, always something
new to talk about . . .
because life never stops bringing you events and circumstances
that demand you ask,
What is the best thing to do here?

————————

From *interpretation,*
let's turn to
incarnation.

In the Gospel of Matthew, a large crowd gathers and Jesus tells
them that he hasn't come
to abolish the Law or the Prophets . . .
but to fulfill them.

Abolishing and *fulfilling* were common ways of speaking about
the Torah in Jesus's day. When people were discussing the Bible
and trying to figure out what it looks like to live it out, if someone
suggested a terrible or misguided interpretation, they would
be told,

You have abolished the Torah!

Or as we might say,
That's missing the point.
Or,
You've lost the plot.
Or,
That's not it.

But if you got it,
if there was some agreement that
yes,
that is what it means,
that's what it looks like to live it out,
then you'd say,
You have fulfilled the Torah!

Because that was the goal—
to take the words and bring them to life.

In your life.

That's the movement in the Bible:
from
word
to
flesh.

That's what we mean by the word *incarnation.*
It's not ultimately about the words—
it's about the powerful, mysterious thing that happens when the
words are acted out in the real world by real people.

So when Jesus comes along and says that he's come to fulfill
the Torah,
he's announcing that he's come to make it speak.
To show what it looks like in actual space and time.
To put a body on it.
To give it legs.

This was both familiar—
people would have understood abolishing and fulfilling language—
and also a bold, radical thing to say.

According to Matthew, Jesus then launches into a series of
teachings that have a pattern to them, a pattern in which he says,
You have heard that it was said . . .
But I tell you . . .

Which was Jesus's way of saying,
You've heard people interpret Torah this way,

but I'm here to tell you
THIS is how to interpret it . . .

And then he offers new interpretations.
Which brings us back to you and me, here and now, reading
the Bible. One of the more compelling questions you can ask
about a topic or theme or idea in the Bible is, What did Jesus say
about it?

For example, violence.
Jesus went to his death on a cross without any violent retaliation.
That's how he reads those passages. He came not to keep violence
in circulation but to bring an end to it. And the most violent books,
like Judges? He never quotes or mentions them.

What about those passages making divisions between this group and
that group?
Whenever there was a group that had been shunned or
marginalized, he intentionally moves toward them. Women,
Samaritans, lepers—he consciously and intentionally steps over
whatever lines have been drawn.

What about those passages naming some people clean and some people
unclean?
He hugs and touches and blesses unclean people. He doesn't
follow the dominant interpretations of his day.

What about all those passages in the Hebrew scriptures that say some
particular group of people was going to be judged harshly by God?
Jesus intentionally mentions a number of those groups, like the
Sidonians, and says they'll be better off than the religious people
who think they're in and the Sidonians are out.

Now, let's take this farther. Because Jesus wasn't just making
new interpretations; he was also claiming that something new

was happening in the life of his people and the world and it was happening *through him.*

In the book of Luke, there's a story about Jesus going back to his hometown to preach a sermon. He goes to the synagogue, where he's asked to read that day's passage—sound familiar?—which is from the prophet Isaiah.

It's a passage about *captives being set free*
and the blind seeing
and the good news being preached to the poor.

The prophet Isaiah has lots of thing to say about a new day coming when a new era would be ushered in by a new kind of leader.

Jesus finishes reading the passage and then says,
Today this scripture is fulfilled in your hearing,
which is another way of saying,
This passage is about me and what I'm up to.

He doesn't say that Isaiah or the Torah or the Law are irrelevant. He says that they've taken on flesh and blood
in him.

Can you see why they take him outside the village and try to kill him?
Those are radical,
bold claims for a rabbi to make.

People often talk about Jesus the master teacher,
Jesus the inspiring role model for social justice,
Jesus the profound mystic with deep insights into the infinite—
but over and over again, he insists that he's doing something far more significant and elemental than all that; he keeps claiming that something new is happening in the world—and it's happening through him.

Something involving heaven and earth coming together,
the divine and the human *in the same place*—
people have described it in lots of different ways.

One of the first followers of Jesus, a man named John, began his
Gospel with this great line:

The Word became flesh and moved into the neighborhood. (The
Message translation)

Can you see the profound questions this raised?
Questions like this one:
Can the divine and the human exist in the same place?

This isn't just a question about him, then—
this is a question about us, now.

Incarnation raises questions about the very nature of what it
means to be human.
*Are we just particular relationships of cells and synapses and blood
and bones?*
Or is there something divine,
something infinite,
something eternal
residing in every one of us?

Are we just dust,
or are we also spirit?

Do you see why incarnation is such a compelling and mysterious and
powerful idea?
Jesus said he came to put flesh and blood on the Torah,
he makes new interpretations,
and then he invites us to enter into the discussion.

Interpretation,
incarnation,
now then, a bit about
invitation.

Jesus tells his disciples at one point that whatever they *bind will be*
bound and whatever they loose will be loosed.

What's he talking about?
Binding and loosing was a first-century way of talking about
interpretation. Jesus tells his followers that it's their turn to make
decisions about what's written in the Bible.

It's as if he says,
You watched me do it.
Now it's your turn.

Figure out what it means to put flesh and blood on it.
In your place,
at your time,
in your world,
figure it out.

He says at one point that it's like someone who keeps bringing new
treasures out of a storehouse.

As in:
You're just scratching the surface.
There's so much more.
You're just getting started.

He even says at another time,

You'll do greater things than these.

Keep engaging,
keep arguing,
keep wrestling,
keep interpreting,
keep dancing with it—
never stop turning the gem.

And then for the rest of the New Testament, what do we see?
His first followers binding and loosing,
discussing and debating,
wrestling and working out what the divine life looks like wherever
they find themselves.

———————

Now, let's look at what happens when one of Jesus's first
followers—a man named Peter—realizes he needs to do some
binding and loosing.

22

The Sheeeeeeet Factor

In the book of Acts, there's a story about a man named Peter who falls into a trance.

Like you do.

But it isn't your ordinary household trance. In this trance Peter sees heaven open up and a sheet come down to earth, and on this sheet are all kinds of animals—the writer is keen for us to know they're four-footed animals as well as reptiles and birds. Peter hears a voice tell him,

Get up, Peter. Kill and eat.

Peter protests with something like,

But I shop at Whole Foods. I make a kale smoothie every morning. I even order that new tofu at Chipotle . . .

Peter protests, saying,

I've never eaten anything impure,

to which the voice responds,

Do not call anything impure that God has made clean.

This happens three times. The sheet is lifted up from where it came, and Peter is left trying to make sense of what just happened.

(By the way, the word used here for *trance* in the original Greek is the word *ekstasis*. From which we get our English word *ecstasy*.)

A bit more about Peter: He was raised in a fishing village called Capernaum. His people were deeply committed to keeping the Torah, which included the parts about avoiding impurity. They understood God to be holy and pure, and they organized their lives around reflecting this purity. These purity laws included food and also *people*. In the same way that you wouldn't touch a dead animal, they also wouldn't touch someone who was considered unclean. Their commitment to being clean was so extensive that they wouldn't even go into the house of someone they considered unclean, which meant anyone who wasn't Jewish. Which meant, basically, *everyone else.*

Now, back to Peter's ecstasy trip.

As soon as his trance is over, there's a knock at the door, and it's some Romans—the ultimate in *unclean*—asking him if he'll come with them to their leader's house. He agrees to go with them, and when he gets there, he tells them that it's against the laws of his people for him to enter the house, and then he says,

But God has shown me that I should not call anyone impure or unclean.

God has shown me?
God has?
How?
How did God show Peter this new truth?

Through a disruption.

Peter had a framework, a paradigm, a way of seeing the world, rooted in his understanding of who God is and what it means to follow God. And central to this understanding was a conviction that some people are clean, and some people are unclean. You can go over to some people's houses, and you can't go over to other people's houses.

But then he has an experience that doesn't fit within that framework. And what is his first reaction to that experience?

Surely not, Lord! I have never eaten anything unclean.

He resists this new understanding.
And what is the basis for his resistance?

His religious convictions!

In the trance God tells him to eat it all, and he argues with God about why he can't eat it all, and his argument is based on his devotion to God. He resists God in the name of . . . God.

It's possible to resist the very growth and change and expanding consciousness that God desires for you by appealing to your religious convictions.

Now, a bit about the nature of growth. New stages of growth, maturity, and consciousness bring with them greater
freedom,

inclusion,
and
complexity.

Before, he couldn't eat it all—now he is free to eat it all.
Before, he had a system of categorizing who is clean and who isn't,
but now all are included.
Before, things were fairly simple: all of humanity can be divided
into clean and unclean. But now, the people he previously thought
were unclean . . . aren't.

Freedom,
inclusion,
complexity.

Next, a bit about disruption. It's disruptions that are often the
catalysts for our growth. You travel, you taste, you meet new
people from other tribes, you read new things, you hear new perspectives, you see data or research you hadn't seen before—and
you discover that your previous ways of categorizing and labeling
and believing aren't adequate.

**You have a choice in that moment: you either ignore or deny or
minimize your experience, or you open yourself up to the very real
pain of leaving that way of understanding behind.**

This is often incredibly exciting and liberating, but it can also have
a traumatic dimension to it, like the carpet is being yanked out
from under you. Like the stable ground you've been walking on for
so long is now trembling.

And yet you can't go back.

Once you've tasted, you can't untaste.

Once you've seen, you can't unsee.

Imagine Peter stepping through the doorway of that Roman's house for the first time. Everything in his upbringing told him that he would be jeopardizing his standing with God to do that, and yet he's now *seen* something new.

And once you've seen, you can't unsee.

My hope is that this brings you tremendous encouragement as you grow and change and see new things. Perhaps you were handed a way of seeing the world (and reading the Bible!) that doesn't work for you anymore, and yet that previous way of understanding still has a strange power over you. Maybe it's the people who taught you that or raised you to think like that or told you that was the only way to see it and if you reject that one understanding, you would suffer.

Or maybe you were marinated in a calm, cool, rational world of evidence and data in which the only things that can be trusted are the facts. You refer to yourself as the logical, rational type who doesn't go for fairy tales. But the truth is, you've had experiences that don't fit into any of your nice, neat, modern categories. You might even use the word *divine*—but not in front of certain friends or family or colleagues.

Wherever you're coming from, don't deny the disruptions.

Don't panic when the room spins, because you've seen something real and life-giving and beautiful and good and hopeful that doesn't fit in any of your boxes.

It's okay. You're not the first. That's how it works. That's how we grow.

Don't fight it.
Enjoy the ecstasy.

It isn't just disruption—it's expansion.
It's the sheeet factor.

Now, let's move from disruptions to all things.

23

All Things Are Yours

All things are yours, whether
Paul or
Apollos or
Cephas or
the world or
life or
death or
the present or
the future—
all are yours,
and you are of Christ,
and Christ is of God.

—1 Corinthians 3

First Corinthians 3 is one of my favorite passages in the Bible.
It starts with the apostle Paul writing his friends in Corinth and
telling them that they're being idiots. My word, not his. *Mere infants*
is how he puts it. He tells them that he gave them milk because
they weren't ready for solid food yet—they're too immature.

Why does he write this?
Because they've been arguing about their favorites.

A bit of background: Paul and his friends have been traveling around telling people about Jesus, stopping in cities like Corinth. Over time, the people in Corinth began to have favorites, some preferring Paul's teaching and some preferring another teacher Apollos's teaching and some liking another teacher Cephas's teaching more.

Their fondness for their particular favorite teacher had become so intense that there was *quarreling and jealousy* among them. This makes Paul mental. I love how he puts it:

For when one says, "I follow Paul," and another, "I follow Apollos," are you not mere human beings?

The obvious answer being: *Uhhhh, yes—we are human beings!* But he's getting after something bigger here: he's calling them to transcend the usual petty ways we divide ourselves. *Back then* people tended to make celebrities out of their leaders, developing allegiances to one and then arguing for why the one they liked is better . . .

waaaaaayyy different than how it is today. (Wink.)

So far fairly straightforward, correct?
These folks in Corinth have taken something good—these teachers coming to their city to help them better understand the way of Jesus—and they've turned it into a source of division and quarreling and jealousy.

But Paul's just getting started.

He then asks,

What, after all, is Apollos?
And what is Paul?

(Please tell me you find that funny. He's writing about himself, right? And he asks, *What is Paul?* He's talking about himself in the third person. Like athletes and rappers do.)

His answer?

Only servants.

And then he adds,

I planted the seed, Apollos watered it, but God has been making it grow.

There's a lot going on here, but at the most basic level, he's calling them out of their division and quarreling by showing them how the divine uses lots of different people to do lots of different things to help us all grow and mature.

He then launches into a long bit about *the grace God has given me* and the foundation that is in Christ and how they are *God's temple.*

(By the way, when someone talks about their body being a temple, the *you*s in the New Testament are *plural.* Paul is writing to a *group* of people, a *body* of believers. So when he says, *you are a temple of God,* he's telling a group of people that *they* collectively are a temple. This would have been an extraordinarily new and powerful idea at a time when the temples of the gods and goddesses were the giant, shiny, magnificent wonders of the world. Paul tells a divisive, flawed group of humans that *they* are where the divine dwells—*what?* Amazing.)

And just when you're deep into a bit about the *foolish* and *wise* of the world, he drops this hammer:

So then, no more boasting about human leaders!

and you realize that all of this has been a brilliant exposition of the problem he started with, which was their petty quarreling over who was their favorite teacher. He's actually been ramping up to deliver this epic crescendo, which begins with:

All things are yours . . .

We could stop right there. It's so good. *All things are yours.* He then adds,

whether Paul or Apollos or Peter. (Cephas, mentioned earlier, is another name for Peter, the one who dreamed about a sheet of unclean-now-clean animals.)

Got it. Brilliant. He's showing them how God uses lots of different people to teach them, and instead of choosing a favorite and then not listening to the others who aren't their favorite, he tells them to claim it all whoever it comes from. All the teachers are theirs. They should enjoy the good and true from whoever it comes from. It's all a gift from God to help them grow.

Why would you cut yourself off from more truth?
Great question. Great point he's making, right?

But then he keeps going. He's not done. Because after the

whether Paul or Apollos or Cephas

part, he adds,

or the world.

The world? The world is yours? So the sentence reads,

*All things are yours, whether Paul or Apollos or Cephas **or the world**. . .*

You see what he's doing here? He starts with their petty jealousies and rivalries, and he grabs them by the shoulders and essentially says, *You're missing it! All of these teachers are gifts from God to help you grow, so don't cut yourself off from what they have to give you by picking favorites and only listening to the one you follow. You're missing out—you're not receiving all God has for you! Claim it all. It's all yours, whatever good that comes your way, whatever truth they help you understand. You've got to see things from a more expanded perspective!*

And then while he's at it, he expands things to include the whole world.

The world is yours, in other words.

What does he mean?
Wherever you find truth, not just through teachers like him and Peter and Apollos, but also whatever helps you grow, however your mind and heart are opened to what God is doing in the world, whatever ways or people or events God uses to teach you truth— affirm it, claim it, own it. It's all yours.

But he's not done.

He then adds,

or life
or death.

Life or death—claim that as well? Life and death are ours? Yes.

And then he adds,

or the present
or the future.

He starts with teachers, then expands to the world. Then he expands it to include being alive or being dead, and then he expands it to include everything that is and everything that will be.

But he's not done, because

all are yours, and you are of Christ, and Christ is of God.

And that ends chapter 3.

My hope is that at this point, you have the sense that you're dancing here in this verse with something very real and very profound and maybe even life changing. It may feel a bit out of grasp, and so let's put some legs on it.

First, when people belittle the Bible as lacking in depth or sophistication, they probably haven't read it. It doesn't matter how smart or educated or studied someone is, to make broad dismissals of the scriptures as having nothing to say to the modern world about what it means to be human is absurd and naïve. This passage here in 1 Corinthians is a layered, eloquent, highly articulate, and wise exploration of how we know and how we think and how we interact with the world.

Second, sometimes we hear people use the phrase *God's truth*. This phrase is a problem. It's best not to use it. Why? Because what other kind of truth is there? If it's true, then it's from God.

Science, art, politics, history, psychology, biology—all truth is God's truth. (A nod to Thomas Aquinas there, as well as Arthur Holmes.) To say something is *God's truth* implies that some truth belongs to God and then there is another kind of truth that apparently doesn't belong to God. Not helpful. If it's true, it has only one source: God.

Third, then, wherever you stumble upon the truth, whoever says it, however you come across it, you affirm it and you claim it because it's yours. This takes us back to Corinth. Paul hears that his friends in Corinth are picking sides, arguing with each other about whose teacher is better, refusing to engage with teachers other than their favorite. He uses this situation to teach them about engaging with the truth wherever they find it, not just through these different teachers but anywhere in the world.

(This is why when people debate faith vs. science they've already missed the point. Faith is about embracing truth wherever it's found, and that of course includes science.)

He's trying to set them free. He wants them to become the kind of people who embrace the truth wherever they find it.

Fourth, this freedom works both ways. We're free to affirm truth wherever we find it, and we're also free to deny that which needs to be denied. If it's wrong or unjust or twisted, we call it whatever it is. This includes religious things, and of course things that go on in churches under the name of Jesus.

Some things that are labeled *Christian* aren't true, and some things that aren't labeled *Christian* are true. Some atheists say lots of things that are true, and some Christians are full of shit.

And then fifth—one more to land this plane—Paul grounds the whole thing in Christ. Paul wants his readers to see that Christ is bigger than any one teacher, any one set of ideas, the world or life or death or the present or the future or anything else you can think of. He wants his friends in Corinth to enjoy the truth wherever they find it, to celebrate it and receive it as the good gift it is from the source of all things, God.

And why does this matter in the world we find ourselves in?
Because religion has given people a lot of categories and labels that simply aren't helpful. Your experience of Christ will consistently transcend whatever boxes you've created, and that includes the Christian religion as well. Paul invites us to become fierce with reality, eyes wide open, affirming what should be affirmed, denying what should be denied, rooted and grounded in the Christ who keeps insisting that all things are ours.

————

One summer I went to a dance performance by Parsons Dance Company. The company was started by David Parsons, one of the premier contemporary choreographers in the world, and the performance was stunning.

Toward the end of the show, there was a solo number. All the lights were turned off except for one white spotlight, which illuminated a male dancer standing alone at the back of the stage. The music began to play, and he began to move, and then something shocking happened—he began to fly.

Not really.

But that's what it *felt* like.

What they did was kill the stage light and turn on a strobe light that pulsed much slower than you usually see a strobe light pulse. When the strobe was *off,* the dancer would run in the pitch-black and jump so that when it pulsed *on,* he'd be in the air, and then it would shut off and he'd land and run and then jump again just before it pulsed on again. From the perspective of the audience, you only saw him when the light was on and he was airborne, appearing and reappearing in different places all over the stage.

The effect was overwhelming.

People began visibly moving in their seats, audibly gasping, and then clapping and cheering but not too much because it was so riveting you barely had energy to do anything else but just stare. You knew there was an explanation—the strobe timing wasn't hard to figure out—but the surprise and shock of it took a person's breath away. Your eyes were watching something you couldn't believe while simultaneously your brain was scrambling to figure out what exactly it was you were watching. The timing of it and the genius of the choreography and the height of his jumps all combined to produce an astonishing experience. So simple, and yet so difficult and so brilliant.

I tell you about that moment because as I type this out, I am well aware of how far my words fall short of giving you the experience I had. I can only point, share, try to explain, doing my best to put language to my experience.

Which takes us to the Bible.

Think about this phrase Paul uses at the end of 1 Corinthians 3: *all things are yours.* It's so big, it's almost too big, right? It's so expansive and massive and inclusive and affirming and buoyant and joyous and positive and embracing and inspiring and uplifting and ballsy and audacious—especially because he's doing it on purpose.
His friends in Corinth have gotten petty, divisive, *small,* stuck in the same old ridiculous debates over who they like more and

who's better and whose side they're on and who they're following and who's more right. He's doing everything he can here to shake them out of their smallness, purposely starting with the divisions among them and calling them to celebrate the truth through whichever teacher it comes—but then he keeps going. Life and death and the world and the present and the future—he appears to be purposely trying to blow their minds with just how much *belongs* to them.

I point this out because a lot of the discussions people have about the Bible are insanely boring. And irrelevant. And distracting. And small.

There's a time and a place for just about any question, but the writers of the Bible wrote these things so that others would experience what they had experienced.

Take this line from Paul in Romans 8:

For I am convinced that neither death nor life, neither angels nor demons, neither the present nor the future, nor any powers, neither height nor depth, nor anything else in all creation, will be able to separate us from the love of God that is in Christ Jesus our Lord.

What does it mean to never be separated from love?
Is that how you live every day?
In every thought, are you constantly reminded that love is the ground of your being?

Paul writes this because in his experience, nothing—and this is a man who was beaten and shipwrecked and had numerous attempts on his life and was betrayed and kicked in the face— nothing could convince him that love is not the deepest reality of the universe.

This is a man who experienced the worst that human beings can do to each other, and his response was not to deny it or say that it wasn't horrible or degrading or to pretend that there weren't times when he wanted to die—his response was to again and again and again and again affirm that there is a love we cannot be separated from.

Is this what people talk about in Bible studies? Because why else would you read the books in this library? You read this book because you want more of *that*, correct? **You want to experience that love and grace and joy, you want it to soak into every pore of your being, and you want to see the world and more specifically your life as a reflection of this love, right?**

Or this line from Paul in Ephesians 3:

And I pray that you, being rooted and established in love, may have power, together with all the Lord's holy people, to grasp how wide and long and high and deep is the love of Christ, and to know this love that surpasses knowledge—that you may be filled to the measure of all the fullness of God.

I love that part—

how wide and long and high and deep is the love of Christ.

Great, isn't it?

He writes because he wants his readers to be *rooted and established in love,* people who are unshakable and courageous and grounded in the reality of this love.

He writes to his friends in Ephesus:

I pray that the eyes of your heart may be enlightened.

When people ask you what the Bible is about, do you answer: *It's about becoming more enlightened?*

Because that's how Paul puts it.

Try this: Repeat the line *All things are yours* like a mantra throughout the day. Write it on the wall or on your hand. When you come across something beautiful, something inspiring, something that moves you, something that grabs hold of your heart, say it to yourself. Let it form grooves in your neural pathways. Let it be the song you're listening to. Let it etch itself on your heart. Let it open up your mind. Let it give you eyes to see what you'd missed until now.

Paul writes because his experience of the resurrected Christ opened him up. It made him bigger and wider and more embracing and full of joy and courageous and filled with wonder and awe.

You can see the world this way.

You have this choice. You have this option. You have this opportunity. You are invited to this. As you go about your day and you face the usual sorts of annoyances and grievances, pay attention to what it's doing to you. Remind yourself that *all things are yours*. Imagine yourself *rooted and established in love*. When you find yourself engaging with people who come from vastly different backgrounds and perspectives, be the first to celebrate whatever is good and true and beautiful in your midst, regardless of where it comes from or who says it or how it arrived there.

All things are yours.

People for thousands of years have had experiences of the divine that left them speechless. Moments when the strobe light kicked in and the dancer appeared to fly and they found themselves fidgeting in their seat, jaw on the ground, blown away.

———————

So what is this movement happening all throughout the pages of the Bible? It's beneath, within, and above everything, like an electricity that the whole thing is plugged in to. Paul calls that Christ.

You see people waking up, leaving things behind, stepping into new realities and something within you resonates, because that's what's happening within you. You read these books and are reminded of your shared human connection with everybody everywhere.

History moves forward, and people are transformed. As Paul says, *the eyes of your heart may be enlightened.*

This is why the Bible has such enduring power. These stories insist in a thousand different ways that we don't have to settle, that tomorrow doesn't have to be a repeat of today, that we don't have to be enslaved to fear or despair—that we can change, move, heal, and we can leave behind whatever needs to be left behind so that we can step into a better future.

24

The Human and the Divine

As you've picked up by now,
the Bible was written by people.

I realize I've said this countless times throughout this book, but I did this on purpose.

I kept repeating this truth that the Bible was written by humans because when you start there, and you go all the way into the humanity of this library of books, you just may find the divine.

And when you do, you will have gotten there honestly.

For example, the resurrection.

There are four accounts of Jesus's life: Matthew, Mark, Luke, and John. They each tell about Jesus being betrayed by one of his friends, having a final meal with his friends, being crucified by the Romans, and then rising from the dead.

If you read these Gospel accounts of Jesus's resurrection, things get very interesting very fast.

Mark reports that on the first day of the week, Mary Magdalene, Mary the Mother of James, and Salome went to Jesus's tomb while
Matthew says it was Mary Magdalene and the other Mary who went to the tomb.

(What's it like to go down in history as *the other* Mary?

Oh you know—it was *the other* Mary.)

According to John's Gospel, it was just Mary Mags, but when she gets to the tomb, some dude asks her why she's crying and who she's looking for, and she thinks it's the gardener so she wants to know, if he's the one who took the body, where did he put it—

Because I will get him
(she says with the force of a woman who is not mucking about).

Then the possible-gardener-dude says her name, and she realizes that it's Jesus.

He's alive?

Luke tells us that this same dude walked with two of the disciples from Jerusalem to Emmaus (which is about seven and a half miles), talking the whole way, and they don't recognize him until they sit down for a meal and he breaks the bread and then they realize it's Jesus.

He's alive?

(Interesting that the people who were closest to Jesus and spent years with him *don't recognize him* post-resurrection. Hmmm. The next time you hear someone insisting that it was an actual, literal resurrection, make sure you add that *bodily* must mean that he didn't look like he looked before.)

One Gospel mentions there was an earthquake—
which the others leave out—
John tells of two angels in white sitting where Jesus's body had been,
Luke says it was two men in gleaming white,
Mark says it was a young man dressed in a white robe *sitting on the right side* of the tomb,
and Matthew says it was an angel of the Lord that rolled back the stone

and then sat on it.
Like you do.
When you roll back a stone.
And open up a tomb.

If you read the accounts back-to-back, there's a lot of running and excitement and general mayhem. Setting aside the issue of whether a man actually rose from the dead (the sheer poetry alone is so crazy good), the four accounts of Jesus rising from the dead contain a number of jumbled details that render that narrative fairly disjointed, to say the least.

There are several responses to these differences:
Some ignore them. They simply repeat again and again that this is God's word and you should take it in faith, you shouldn't question its truth, etc.
Others take these differences as clear and tangible proof of its susceptibility. See? It's all myth, fable, miracle, fantasy, etc., borrowed from the tales of the day.

I find both perspectives boring.

Before I explain, though, a few thoughts about propaganda.

To summarize, this is the worst propaganda. Ever. If you're trying to start a religion, this is a crap way to do it. How are you going to inspire confidence if you can't even report the details accurately with one voice?

Not to mention the women, which we will mention because the Gospel writers all mention the women. In these accounts, the writers all affirm that it's the women who first realized (say it with me now):

He's alive!

In the first century, women didn't have much in the way of respect as we think of it, so their word meant next to nothing in court. Why, in a culture that had such little regard for the witness of women, would you tell a story that hinges to a large degree on the witness of women?

Second, Matthew writes that Jesus met up with his crew on a mountain in Galilee, and

when they saw him, they worshipped him; but some doubted.

Wha . . . ? They *doubted*?

Why would Matthew include this?

If the point of your book is that Jesus is the Messiah, the King, the long-awaited Savior of the World, the one everybody has been waiting for, why would you reach the crescendo of the story and then include a line about some of his followers doubting? Doesn't that ruin the moment? Doesn't this undermine everything you've been saying in your story?

That said, a question for you:
If something extraordinary did happen, how would it be remembered?

Which leads to another question:
If someone did rise from the dead, how would that story be told?
In a calm and collected and polished manner, or in a slightly
haphazard way that buzzed and hummed and rattled with the
electricity that comes from experiencing something so unexpected
and extraordinary that you don't really have categories for it?

Which leads to another question:
Is the haphazard humanity of it all reason to dismiss it or signs that
it's an authentic record of what happened?

Which leads to another question:
When Matthew tells us that some of Jesus's followers doubted,
does this undermine the story, or is this the exact kind of honesty
that reflects how people actually are?

When each of the Gospel writers includes the part about the
women being witnesses, why risk it? What a strange thing to
include knowing it would discredit their story, *unless women actually
were the first witnesses.*

How open-minded are you?
What's possible?
Is there a new creation bursting within this one?
Did something happen that changes everything?
Is the tomb empty?
What happens if you actually live like it's true?
What does this story do to your heart?

For some, the Bible is just a collection of old books. Books written
by people and nothing more. For others, the Bible is a collection of

books, but it's also more than just a collection of books. They're books, but they're more than just books.

Why do the four resurrection accounts in the Gospels differ on basic details?
Why aren't there any clear denunciations of polygamy? Or slavery?
Why does Paul say in the New Testament that it's him speaking, *not the Lord*?

When people charge in with great insistence that this is God's word all the while neglecting the very real humanity of these books, they can inadvertently rob these writings of their sacred power.

All because of starting in the wrong place.

You start with the human. You ask those questions, you enter there, you direct your energies to understanding why *these* people wrote *these* books.

Because whatever divine you find in it, you find the divine *through* and *in* the human, not around it.

Part 3

Where That Something Takes Us

So what does it look like to read the Bible this way?

That's the question, right?

Because it's one thing to cover the ground we have so far in this book and see the pull, the call, the tug, the Spirit moving things forward in the Bible, raising profound questions, drawing us into a bigger and better future.

It's another to see that same thing happening in the world around you.

Which takes us back to the question:

So how do you do it?
To get at this,
a few examples—
one about technology,
one about apocalypse,
one about the art of subversion,
and then we'll get to America.

25

Babel

In Genesis 11, we read the story of the Tower of Babel. People decide they're going to build a tower that reaches to heaven

so that we may make a name for ourselves; otherwise we will be scattered over the face of the whole earth,

but God comes and inspects what they're doing and decides that if they can do this,

nothing they plan to do will be impossible for them,

and so God decides,

Come, let us go down and confuse their language so they will not understand each other.

End of story.

A couple of questions:

First, who built Babel?
If we go back one chapter, we read,

Cush was the father of Nimrod, who became a mighty warrior on the earth. He was a mighty hunter before the LORD. . . . The first centers of his kingdom were Babylon [also known as Babel], Uruk, Akkad . . .

What else do we know about Nimrod?
(Besides being one of the best Green Day albums? I couldn't resist that one.) The name Nimrod comes from the Hebrew root word for *rebel*. Interesting.

Why does this matter?
Because by the time you get to the story about the Tower of Babel, what we know is that it's being built by a very, very violent and powerful warrior who is also building lots of other cities and that his name is connected with the idea of rebelling. This is called *empire building*. It's what happens when someone, or a group of people, use military might and economic dominance to crush anything—and anyone—in the way of their plans.

Are there any other details we may have missed in our earlier readings of this story?
Yes. What was it exactly they said to each other about *how* they were building the tower?
The text reads,

They said to each other, "Come, let's make bricks and bake them thoroughly." They used brick instead of stone, and tar for mortar.

These details are huge. They used brick instead of stone. Have you tried to build something tall out of stone? It's next to impossible. Why? Because stones are round and often smooth and all different shapes and sizes, and they're hard to stack on top of each other. Total hassle.

But this is a story about bricks. *Someone invented the brick.* You can make bricks the same size, the same shape—you can make bricks to exact specifications for whatever it is you are trying to build. Like a tower.

If you'd been building things with stone for, like, forever, and then you started using bricks, what questions would you immediately have?

Probably questions along the lines of:

These bricks are amazing. They make all kinds of building possible that wasn't possible before—just how big could we make something with these new bricks?

But in the story, it isn't just bricks they're building with. They're also using tar for mortar. Mortar is like cement, helping the bricks stick together.

What's another name for these details about the brick and mortar?
Technology! This is a story about, among other things, technology. Someone invented something new—the brick and mortar—which allowed people to make and do things they hadn't been able to do before.

And what does *that* have to do with Nimrod?
This is a story about what happens when a powerful warrior who's building an empire gets his hands on new technology and begins to use it to set himself up as a god, crushing everybody and everything in his path.

And what does that tell us about the world the author of this story was living in?
This was a new phenomenon. People were spreading and scattering and settling in new places, and some were gaining more and more power and influence, which affected everybody else. (When-

ever you hear someone say that corporations and banks on Wall Street have gotten too powerful, you are hearing echoes of the same sentiment, thousands of years later.) The story reflects a growing awareness and concern that there is a higher good for humanity than the strong dominating the weak, the powerful crushing the powerless, the proud raising themselves up to godlike status. Imagine building little walls out of stone your entire life and then making a trip to Babel and seeing people starting work on a tower made of bricks. It may have been awe inspiring, but we can also assume that it would have been *terrifying*. If somebody can do *that,* what else can they do? Or to put more of an edge on it, *what couldn't they do?* (Imagine if other countries had nuclear bombs but your country didn't. And imagine what it would be like to not have nuclear bombs but to know that one of those countries that did have nuclear bombs had actually used their nuclear bombs in recent history, dropping those bombs on actual cities that people lived in. Terrifying.)

What does this story tell us about what it means to be human?
We have tremendous power and ability as humans. We can invent things and build things and dream things up and then make them. It's extraordinary, and it's to be celebrated and enjoyed. (Say it with me now: HD flat screen. Chipotle. Almond Surfboards. Anything made by Apple. Rickenbacker guitars. I could go on. So could you.) We also have the tremendous capacity to use our energies and minds and power and abilities to further our own purposes through greed and empire building at the expense of those around us, making the world less and less of a peaceful place where everybody is thriving.

And what does that have to do with today?
For many people, the Bible is a book about a long time ago that spells out how the world is going to end in the future when people leave this world to go somewhere else.
It's understood to be a book about

then—the past
or
then—the future,
but many haven't ever read it as a book about *now.*

This story here about the Tower of Babel has enduring power
because of its reminder that we're building the world. We're
creating something. We're doing something with our minds and
energies and money and technology. And what we're doing, with
fossil fuels and nuclear bombs and poisoned water sources and
factories belching smoke into the air, is threatening the future of
the world. To read this story as a story about back then is to miss
its power for us here and now.

It's a story, but it's also a warning.

We have this tremendous capacity to invent and innovate and
create, and that power can be used for good—to care for each
other and the world. And it can also be used in destructive ways to
oppress and dehumanize others.

This ancient story is actually happening right now . . . which means
we need to talk about apocalypse.

26

Two or Three Kinds of Apocalypses

Let's talk about the end of the world for a minute. For a lot of people, the point of the Bible is that the world is going to end at some point in the future, and it's really important that you're on the right team when the apocalypse comes.

But there are two or three kinds of apocalypses.
In the first kind of apocalypse, the world as we know it ends suddenly because of something catastrophic and unexpected.
There are *natural* versions of this fear in which a meteor hits earth or a disease spreads unchecked or an earthquake causes the oceans to flood the continents until humanity is no more. There are also *divine* versions in which God gets so fed up with humans making a mess of things that God finally says, *Enough!* and shows up to right the wrongs and bring judgment and clean some house.

This understanding of apocalypse taps into a very specific human fear: that out of nowhere something could happen tomorrow that would end life as we know it.
The shock and unexpected terror of this possibility has spawned countless comics, novels, and of course movies.

You know the ones, where Bruce Willis shows up at the last minute to save the day. Or Will Smith.

In the religious version, you'll often hear that when this happens, one group heads to a good place, and the rest of humanity heads to a bad place. (The people who tell this version of the story are always in the good group, coincidentally enough.) And so your job is to get as many people inside the tent/club/religion/group as possible so that when that day comes, you can all escape together and go somewhere else.

One more observation about this kind of apocalypse: **In this version the end of the world/last days/end times are generally seen as something that is out of our control.** We can't control the timing, the dates, or the particular details. We're passive participants, helpless to control the *when* of it, hoping to escape the worst.

Now, a second kind of apocalypse.
The second kind of apocalypse is the kind that we bring on ourselves. This one comes about because we humans have made a mess of the earth through our consumption of fossil fuels and nuclear bombs and carbon footprints and chemicals dumped in oceans and rivers and lakes. Icebergs melt and water sources are contaminated, wildlife decimated, rain forests leveled—**this kind of apocalypse is the kind that we can control.** It comes because we didn't take our divine responsibility to be stewards of creation seriously enough. It happens because we ignored the evidence, we laughed at the people who warned us, and we refused to make the difficult changes needed to live in the world more sustainably.

The good news about this kind of apocalypse, of course, is that we can change our ways, reform our habits, pass new laws, adopt new technologies, live more sustainably, pollute less—the list goes on and on.

(It's important to note here that in the Genesis poem that begins the Bible, the relationship of the people to the soil—to their *environment*—is of utmost importance. Why? Because our very survival depends on it.)

My point with these two kinds of apocalypses?
Some people have tremendous concern about the apocalypse we
can't **control and nowhere near enough concern for the one we**
can **control.**

Instead of speculating about the end times and writing terrible novels about people being left behind and preaching ridiculous sermons connecting Iran to the book of Daniel, it's better if people agree that we aren't going to worry about what we can't control and we are going to become far more intentional about what we can control—loving our neighbor, becoming people of character and integrity, taking better care of the earth. What if all that anxiety and fear and concern about apocalypse (that has sold a ton of movie tickets) was channeled into actual change?

The story we read in the Bible is about this world, our home. Jesus didn't talk about a God who wants to burn this place down and take us somewhere else; he talked about the renewing of this place, the only home we've ever had. Central to the story of the Bible is the affirmation of trees and seas and rocks and air and soil and blood and sweat and skin and all the materiality and diversity and creativity that we know to be central to our life in this world. Jesus talked about a coming time when God would restore and renew and reconcile and redeem and make things right, and he invites us to anticipate that day by doing our part to bring heaven to earth, here, now, today.

Which brings us to a third kind of apocalypse. The word *apocalypse* literally means *uncovering* or *unveiling* or *disclosing*. **A true apocalypse is about things being revealed for what they actually are.**

Like in 2 Peter in the New Testament, where Peter writes that

the earth and everything done in it will be laid bare.

The phrase *laid bare* in the Greek is the word *heurisko*—it means to find or learn or discover. (It's where we get the word *eureka!*, which feels like it needs an exclamation point, doesn't it?)

When the writers of the Bible wrote about this laying bare, it was with the anticipation of everything being made right, put back in place, restored. It was a hopeful, buoyant, joyous expectation that there is still a better future for the world.

And so every time you act in anticipation of that, you're taking part in the future *now*.

So when Peter writes,
You ought to live holy and godly lives as you look forward to the day of God and speed its coming,
that's actually an apocalyptic verse.

What?
Speed its coming?
We can affect the future.
We can participate in bringing about a new world.
Us.
Right now.

A true apocalypse isn't something to be feared but something to be celebrated. And entered into. Now.

27

The Book of Revelation, of Course

A mulatto
An albino
A mosquito
My libido
Yeah!

—Kurt Cobain

Now, let's take an apocalyptic book in the Bible—the book of Revelation—and let's ask the question: What does this book have to say to us now?

So, a bit about the book of Revelation.

First, the book of Revelation is a letter.
It's written from a pastor named John to his congregation.
His people are facing very difficult challenges, and John writes to them to encourage them to stay strong and keep going.

His letter is about real people getting real help in the midst of really trying times.

Second, his people were surrounded with propaganda proclaiming the Roman Emperor as a god on earth. From the market to the arena to statues to coins, everywhere they turned they were confronted with proclamations of how great and powerful and good the Emperor Caesar was who ruled the empire.
One Caesar—Domitian—had a choir that followed him everywhere he went, singing,

You are worthy, our Lord and God,
to receive glory and honor and power.

When the Caesar held Olympic games in the arena, he would begin by addressing the leaders of the various provinces, telling them what he thought they were doing well and what they needed to change or he would deal with them severely.

This was life in the empire.

The Roman Empire had conquered the world by marching into new territory and demanding that people confess,

Caesar is Lord.

If you did submit, you then became citizens of the Roman Empire.
If you didn't, if you didn't want to become citizens, or you didn't believe Caesar is Lord, you were conquered anyway. And those who resisted were often hung on crosses to show everyone what happened when you resisted the empire.

Central to this conquest of the world was the belief that military victory is peace.

There was even one line from the empire propaganda that went

*Caesar is the son of God sent to earth to bring about a universal reign
of peace and prosperity.*

You see the problem here, right?

It's only peace if you're holding the sword; to all those who
were conquered by this devastating war machine—and hung on
crosses—it wasn't peace.

It was awful.
It was oppressive.
It was evil.

Third, then, it's important to understand that John's people have a
different vision for the world, because they believed that Jesus was
Lord. They were part of a movement—a resistance movement—
rooted in the conviction that the world isn't made better through
military violence but through compassion and sacrificial love.

They saw Jesus as the anti-Caesar.
Better to die on a cross at the hands of the empire than perpetuate
the endless cycle of violence like the Romans.

So imagine you're a cabbage farmer,
and you're part of this new anti-empire Jesus movement,
and you take your load of cabbages to the market and before they'll
let you sell your cabbages, you have to offer incense to Caesar.

What do you do?

Caesar claimed to be God, and in Jewish thinking anyone who
claimed to be a god was like a beast, so to offer incense would be
taking the mark of the beast.

Do you offer the incense?

Because if you don't, then how are you going to sell your cabbages and get the money you need to provide for your family?

These were the kinds of dilemmas the people in John's congregation would have been facing as Jesus followers under the boot of the empire.

Which leads us back to the letter he writes his people.

John is also a poet.

And in this letter, good and evil are in conflict.
According to John, there is actual evil in the world, and it is opposed to human thriving. This evil is not a fantasy or an idea or an abstract concept; it is real and torments people in a number of ways. John uses a number of images to portray this evil as the haunting, destructive, insidious reality that it is.

John uses a number of graphic, violent images and scenes in his letter because that's how life is.
Imagine lying in a hospital bed recovering from chemotherapy, wondering how many days of living you have left, and a chaplain comes in and smiles and tells you that life is like a box of chocolates. This is not helpful, right? With whatever strength you can muster, you grab the chaplain by the lapels, and you say in a low growl, *Enough with the damn chocolates!* Or something like that. Why? Because when people talk about cancer, they talk about *fighting* and *battling* and *hanging on for dear life*.
If you're living in a country right now where military groups are coming through villages, setting homes on fire, and violating the helpless, **you need encouragement—but it has to be encouragement that matches in intensity the evil that you are experiencing,** right?

Now, here's what's so brilliant about the book of Revelation. John begins his letter by having Jesus address the leaders of the various churches in the region. Jesus tells them what they're doing well and then he tells them what they need to do better.

Sound familiar?

That's how Caesar began his games in the arena!

John then describes the throne of God where angels are singing . . . wait for it . . .

You are worthy, our Lord and God,
to receive glory and honor and power.

Sound familiar?
That's what Caesar's choir sang about him.

What is John doing here?
He's taking the theater and propaganda and slogans and pomp of the empire and he's subverting it.

It's as if he's telling his people
Don't fall for the lie.
Don't be seduced by the power of the empire.
There's a better way.

What is Revelation? Satire.
Political, dangerous, pointed, sharp satire.

But it isn't just satire.

He then tells about how he saw the throne of God and there was a lamb that had been slain—remember, the Romans did a lot of slaying—

all of it to essentially say

I've seen who's in charge of the world . . .
and it's not Caesar!

That's the power of this letter.
John reminds his people that ruling, military, oppressive power like
that of the empire is temporary and passing. It can't endure.

**John uses this imagery because he believes that in Jesus, God has
decisively dealt with evil.**
He writes to them of a reality beyond their everyday circumstances,
a reality rooted in God's love for all of creation. He writes to
them of the life they have in Christ even if their present, physical,
earthly life may come to an abrupt end. He wants his people to
find comfort and peace in the turmoil raging around them, and he
believes this is found in Jesus, who can be trusted.

I remember the first time I heard "Smells Like Teen Spirit" by
Nirvana. I was in my last year of college, I was living in a house with
my friends, and Steve Huber told me he wanted to play me a song
by this new band Nirvana. We went into his room, and he put in
the cassette (!), and when that first chorus kicked in, we looked at
each other and said, *This is amazing. I've never heard anything like
this before. It's so raw and honest, it's unnerving.*

Remember hair metal? That was the music on the radio at
the time—Poison, Ratt, Warrant, Whitesnake, Bon Jovi—shiny
music by men with large, permy hair. And then along came Kurt
Cobain from Seattle *in a cardigan!* And he's slightly hunched over,
and he's kind of slurring the words, and he's howling from the
depth of his being.

It was like getting hit by a freight train.

It was real.

You felt it in your bones. All that angst and tension and heartbreak and confusion, right there in one song. And those lyrics:

> A mulatto
> An albino
> A mosquito
> My libido
> Yeah!

Imagine if I were to ask you what the words literally mean. Albino? Mosquito?

You'd say the literal meaning isn't the point, it's poetry, and it's a series of fragments that are better *felt* than *analyzed,* right? You'd tell me that the power of that music—all music, actually— comes from how it speaks to the heart. How it reminds you you're not alone, how it gives sound and words to sensations and feelings.

So does that mean there's nothing historical in the book of Revelation? No, it's a real pastor, living in a real place, at a real time, living under a real government, writing to real people in his real church with real struggles and challenges.

It's just that sometimes, a poem is as real as you can be.

One of the things people often mention about the book of Revelation is how much violence there is. This observation is often made with surprise, sometimes shock, and often a bit of repulsion. *It's just so bloody . . .*

But then people sit in a movie theater and watch The Lord of the Rings *for three hours, and they aren't repulsed—they're inspired. They wait expectantly for the next two films in the series to be released. They buy the box set.*

———————

For some, the primary way they were taught the book of Revelation is that it's about the future, about things that haven't happened yet. And so the questions are generally about the end of the world, the role of whatever country happens to be the biggest threat to their country at the moment, and the big one:

Are we living in the last days?

It's important to note here that a brief look at movies that have been released over the past decade reveals that these aren't just religious people's questions—lots of people wonder about the end of the world.

A couple of questions about those questions:
Let's say a friend of yours lives in Syria in the next village over from a village that recently experienced a chemical weapons attack— what kind of letter do you write your friend?

Do you write her about things that are going to happen in thousands of years?

Or do you show her a letter like Revelation, which condemns evil and calls out the injustice of those who use their power to oppress others and inspires all those in the thick of the struggle to stay strong and not lose heart because love is a stronger force than anything aligned against it?

28

Why Americans Often Miss the Major Themes of the Bible

The Bible was written by Jewish people who belonged to a Jewish minority living under the oppression of a succession of massive military superpowers who had conquered them:

The Egyptians,
the Persians,
the Babylonians,
the Assyrians,
the Greeks,
the Romans.

These people had experienced defeat generation after generation after generation. You can see why the crowds want to make Jesus into a king who will liberate them. **They've been conquered by one empire after another for hundreds and hundreds of years, and they want it to end. They want to be free.**

They're tired of being oppressed.

The writers of the Bible were from a tribe that had been on the receiving end of an untold amount of suffering and hardship at the hands of powerful, dominant nations. And so they write with particular vehemence toward those who abuse their power and take advantage of people weaker than they are.

We see this theme emerging again and again in the Bible.
What will you do with your power and wealth and might and armies?
What kind of world will you create with it?
Will you use it to manipulate and overpower others to build your empire even bigger, or will you use it to help the widow, the orphan, and the refugee among you?

There's a great story in the book of 1 Kings about the queen of Sheba coming to visit King Solomon. She tours his gardens and palace and sees his servants and food and wealth, and then she tells him she knows why he's been so blessed:

to maintain justice and righteousness.

She essentially says,

I know why your God has given you this—to take care of everybody on the underside.

Solomon, however, doesn't do this. He builds a temple to God using slave labor. He establishes military bases. He becomes an arms dealer.

He uses his wealth and power to dominate others and expand his kingdom, at the expense of the poor and needy in his midst.

He loses the plot.
He becomes indifferent.
He's the new Pharaoh.

He can't hear the cry.

And so Solomon dies, and a succession of kings follows him, and they slowly bring about the unraveling of the kingdom.

Because when you can't hear the cry, when you stop caring for the widow, the orphan, and the refugee among you, it always leads to the diminishing of your empire.

History is usually told by the strong, who, with great flourish, tell you about all of those they conquered and all the brave acts they did.

But the Bible is different. The Bible writers relentlessly critique those kinds of stories. Empires always need propaganda to keep expanding. They need a myth, a story, a narrative that justifies their endless hunger for more soldiers, more victory, more wealth and power. And these writers of the Bible know that underneath all that propaganda will be an animating myth that justifies the bombs and drones and violence.

And they condemn it,
again and again and again.

Can you see why Americans often miss some of the central themes of this book?

Can you see how citizens of the most powerful global military superpower the world has ever seen might miss some of the themes of a library of books written by people under the rule and domination of the military superpowers of their day?

In the Psalms, it's written:
Some trust in chariots . . .
but we trust in the name of the LORD our God . . .

The chariot was the tank or the fighter jet of the ancient world.
When you don't have as many chariots (or tanks or guns or fighter jets) as whoever is conquering you at the moment, you have to look beyond your own strength, and beyond the strength of your oppressor, for hope and consolation. You have to trust that there are larger forces at work in the universe, forces that are on your side.

Do you see why this Psalm was such a comfort to these people?

Do you see why you may miss the power of this Psalm
when you're the one with the chariots?

———————

I was born in America, raised in America, and I've lived my whole life in America.

And I'm grateful for that.
Freedom, rights, the chance to pursue your dreams—great.

But America isn't just a nation;
it's also a system.

A system shaped by capitalism and democracy and corporations and convictions and a particular spirit that from the birth of America has been whispering in her ear

more.

More land,
more expansion,
more wealth,
more power.

More influence,

more customers,
more square footage,
more product for less money,
more up and to the right.

When in doubt, *more*,
because more is better.

But *more* is not always better.
More is not always good.
Sometimes more is bad. Destructive. Wrong. And sometimes it's
downright evil.

Which takes us back to the Bible,
because one of the central themes of the Bible is the critique
of *more*.

This is what we read, again and again in the pages of the Bible—
fearless, pointed, courageous, subversive, poetic, sometimes
sarcastic, other times angry, heartfelt, razor-sharp critique of people,
nations, systems, and empires endlessly accumulating more at the
expense of everybody they're stepping on along the way.

The power of the Bible for people like us living in times like these
is that it shows us what it looks like to resist what needs to be
resisted and critique what needs to be critiqued while holding on
to the conviction that there is a sacred mystery at the heart of
being human.

Because that's the temptation, right?
To become cynical, jaded, weary.

To see all the injustice and hypocrisy and abuse and exploitation
and just want to give up.
To see how the system is rigged, and check out.

And yet, there's this library of books,
written thousands of years ago,
that is unrelenting in its insistence that it matters how we respond
to the world we find ourselves in.
It matters what we do.
It matters what we believe.
It matters how we think about our lives and the world around us.
It matters how we treat each other.

How do you stand up against injustice and not lose hope?
How do you live with less worry and more joy?
How do you forgive someone who has wronged you?
What do you do when the person in power doesn't have any
integrity or moral compass?
When do you take action and when do you trust that it's all going
to work out?

What we see in the Bible is that we aren't alone in these questions—
these are the questions people have been wrestling with for
thousands of years. And on page after page after page of their
writings they never stop insisting that this struggle we call life isn't
futile, hopeless, or pointless. It's divine.

Part 4

The Questions That Always Come Up

So there.
We're done. That's it.
That was my book on the Bible.
I hope it helps you read the Bible in a whole new way.

That said, what I've learned is that anytime you talk about the Bible, people have questions.

Lots of them. Lists of them. Weird ones. Strange ones. Questions I would never have thought of in a thousand years that have been keeping people awake at night.

So just to keep it real, let's look at a few of the most common I've heard over the years.

29

Why Are There All Those Genealogies?

Let's start with the one that begins Matthew's Gospel. Matthew starts with the claim that this is the genealogy of Jesus, the son of David, then lists lots of dudes (including several women, which was atypical for the day) culminating with Jesus. (By the way, the women he mentions and their stories? There are a thousand sermons in there.)

Jesus, the son of *David*.
Interesting, because David has the mathematical value of . . . fourteen.

You with me?
No?
Okay, then, a bit of background.

Numbers were very important to the Hebrews. So much so that words were understood for what they referred to but also for their numerical value. How did they get that?

I'll do it in English first.

A is the first letter, so it's a one.
B is the second letter, so it's a two.
C is three, and so on.
The word *cab,* then, in English, would be
3+1+2, which would give it the numerical value of six.

In Hebrew, the name *David* is the letters D-V-D (no vowels in
Hebrew). *D* is the fourth letter, and *V* is the sixth.
D-V-D, then, is 4+6+4, which is fourteen.

The name *David* has the numerical value of fourteen.

Why do I show you this?
Take a look at Matthew's genealogy. You're bored, right? It's just a
list of names. What a brutal way to begin a book.

Unless you count how many names there are.

What you'll quickly notice is that the names are actually grouped,
and they're grouped in fourteens. Why is this significant? Because
Matthew is writing to a Jewish audience, an audience who had
been waiting for the son of David to appear and save them. And
everyone knew that David's name equaled fourteen. So right out
of the gate, the intentional groupings would have been shouting,
"Fourteen! Fourteen! Fourteen!" to Matthew's readers.

The text continues:
Thus were there fourteen generations in all from Abraham to David,
fourteen from David to the exile in Babylon, and fourteen from the exile
to the Messiah.

David, David, David.
Fourteen. Fourteen.

Why is Matthew writing this book?

His original Jewish audience would have already known just from the genealogy—

Matthew believes Jesus is the son of David we've been waiting for, and he's writing to tell us why . . .

(By the way, fourteen is two of what? Seven. Exactly. And seven is a hugely significant number in the Bible. What does the Torah say about establishing the truth of something? That it takes two witnesses. So fourteen is two sevens, which adds another layer to Matthew's genealogy. He's saying that all those names in that list are acting as witnesses to Jesus being the Messiah, like in court, according to the Torah.)

Now, from Matthew, let's turn to Luke, who also has a genealogy but his doesn't start way back in time and move forward. His starts with Jesus and moves backward. Matthew traces Jesus through Joseph and his father's line to Abraham. Luke doesn't do this. He says Jesus

was the son, so it was thought, of Joseph

and then proceeds to trace Jesus's line through his *mother*. And he doesn't stop—he goes all the way back to Adam the son of . . . God.

Why?

Great question.

Which raises another question: Who is Luke writing to?

Because Matthew had his Jewish tribe in mind. Luke, on the other hand, is writing for a much broader audience. So proving Jesus's

Jewish cred wouldn't help his story much, but Jesus being the son of all humanity—now, that had weight in Luke's world.

He's telling a big story about the salvation of all humanity through this Jewish Jesus, so he's trying to get his audience to see the worldwide humanity of Jesus. To do this, he takes Jesus's bloodline where you'd naturally take it if that was the aim of your story.

Was it unusual to trace a man's genealogy through his mother's side?

Yes, it was. Because what does Luke continually show us? The Jesus who is for everybody, is found among the poor, goes to the edge, the margins, and embraces the least and unexpected. He is the one who tells stories about lost coins, lost sheep, and lost sons.

Can you see how each of their genealogies is used to serve a larger purpose in their writing? The factual accuracy in both cases is secondary to a larger *theological* point they're both making. This is important, because if you make the facts the point, and whether or not their genealogies are precisely correct, you're looking for something that wasn't the first intention of the writers.

From Luke's genealogy, let's go further back and pick another one, how about the one that starts in 1 Chronicles? It just keeps going . . . and going . . . and going, name after name.

Ziph,
Ziphah,
Soko,
Ziklag,
Ophrah,
Kenaz,
Iru,
Naam,

Guni,

Anub,

and of course Peleg, who you're all familiar with, who was named Peleg because in his time the earth was divided. (You can't make this up. Chapter 1, verse 19. You remember that time, right? *When the earth was divided?* Good times.)

What is the point of all these lists of names? Once again, a great question, one that is answered when you ask,

What is the story they're telling?

It's a story about a tribe, a new kind of tribe, a tribe that would bless all the other tribes. Remember, all of the tribes had their gods and goddesses. That was how things were. And when you traveled to a new place, you would ask about the god of that region because each tribe had their gods and each region had its gods. But this tribe was different. This tribe believed that there was *one* God who was the source of all life, *one* God who was good and loved everybody and wanted to bless everybody through their tribe. Living this out was obviously something they had a difficult time doing, but the idea was deep in their bones. So being a part of this tribe was important, and passing on the legacy of the tribe (having kids) was one of the most important ways you honored the tribe.

The story, after all, began with a man named Abraham who had *faith*, we're told. Faith that a better world was possible, faith that God was up to something in this battered and broken world, faith that he had a role to play in the new thing God was doing.

Who was Abraham again?

Oh that's right—nobody.

In the ancient Near East, you recorded genealogies to show how you were the preeminent people, you were the best, you were the first, you were the most important. (Sumerian, Egyptian, etc., genealogies were giant exercises in reminding people of your greatness.)

But Abraham—Abraham was a nobody.
And those long lists of dudes who begat dudes who begat dudes?

Nobodies. Average Joes. Or maybe we should say average Arphaxads. Average Jobabs. Average Nahors.

The people who wrote these lists believed that the God of the universe, the singular source of life, was at work within human history through really normal, average people to redeem the whole thing.

And so those lists were a way of saying,
and he was faithful
and his son was the real thing
and his son stayed the course
and his son did the right thing
and his son was faithful . . .

(Two side notes for those of you who love the details:
First, in the Torah it was commanded that if your brother dies, you marry his wife to keep the bloodline going. That's why some of the genealogies don't line up to the modern mind; they're recording complicated arrangements because of brothers dying but their bloodlines continuing through their brothers marrying their wives. Second, remember that ancient understandings of biology were fairly limited. They observed that a woman didn't get pregnant unless she'd been with a man; so they concluded that a man must be the one who possesses the seed, so to speak, of life. From this they deduced that the bloodline is furthered by the man, hence the long lists of dudes.)

To the original audience of these stories and the genealogies in them, those lists weren't boring; they were inspiring. *God uses nobodies.*

And how do you acknowledge the role a nobody played in the redemption of all things?

You write down their name.
And you remember them.
And you thank God for them.
And you vow to do your part to carry on the tradition.

So you may skip them,
and wonder why they're there,
and pick them apart for their accuracy or lack of it,
but for the original audience,
those long lists—and the longer the better—were signs of hope.

Hope that nobody is forgotten, hope that average people living normal lives, not known for being heroes or coming from wealthy families or having royal blood, were all a part of something bigger than themselves.

30

Why Is Leviticus
in the Bible?

Leviticus begins with extensive instructions on how to offer five
different sacrifices—the burned offering, the grain offering, the
peace offering, the sin offering, and the guilt offering.

To add to that, there's verse after verse of instructions on what to
do with the fat (of the animal you're offering), the loins (of said
animal), the long lobe of the liver (of the person—I'm just messing
with you . . .), and the blood. Of the animal. Lots and lots of blood.

Two notes about the text:
First, the book begins with the LORD (this name for God is
intimately connected with the God who rescues people from
whatever they're enslaved to) telling Moses to tell the people,

When anyone among you brings an offering to the LORD . . .

The word for *offering* here in the Hebrew language is the word
corban, and it means *to draw near*.

Draw near?

Let's get some context. The gods at that time were understood to be distant, detached, demanding, and constantly needing to be appeased. You never knew where you stood with the gods.

But this God—you can draw near to this God? You can? That was a new idea.

A pause to reflect. **We are one verse in, and minds are being blown.** People didn't talk about the gods like this. People didn't conceive of the gods like this.

This God is different.
You can come near to this God.
You can relate to this God.

Which leads to a second observation about the text: One of the offerings is called the *peace* offering. It's an offering that you give because you have peace with God. One of the instructions in chapter 7 regarding this peace offering is that the meat that you offered

must be eaten on the day it is offered.

What's it called when you eat something? (Not a trick question.)

It's called a meal.

You come near to this God, and then you have a meal celebrating the peace that you have with this God.

In other words, you can know where you stand with this God.

But what if you suddenly realize that you did something wrong several days ago—how do you make things right? There was an offering for that.

What if you did something unintentional that ended up harming someone but you only just now found out about it? There was an offering for that.

What if you had a deep sense of anxiety in your conscience from something you felt guilty about? There was an offering for that as well.

But why all the endless details?
People believed that the gods could smite you at any moment for an improper gesture or a sacrifice offered carelessly. That's how people saw the gods. One screwup and you're done. The details would have had a significant calming effect, reassuring you that you're doing it correctly and not bringing unnecessary judgment on yourself.

And a much deeper level at the heart of Leviticus is the insistence that human action matters. That it is holy. That there is weight and significance to what people do in the world. In a time and place where human life was fragile and fleeting, and people were often victims of great violence, to insist on the dignity and holiness of human action was a revolutionary idea.

Why all the repetition that makes it so hard to read through the book without dozing off?
Good point. Why didn't they just refer to their iPads? Actually, the answer is in the question: Culture was primarily oral at this point. The repetition made it easier to memorize and then hand down to the next generation.

Why didn't they just skip the whole sacrificial system all together?
That would have been amazing. Just scrap the whole thing. Announce that the final sacrifice has been offered and there's no more need to do such things. Declare that the temple is going to be torn down. Proclaim that it is finished. Oh wait, we're getting

ahead of ourselves, aren't we? (Please tell me you enjoyed that last paragraph.)

So why didn't they skip it?

Well, how do you change things? How does consciousness change and evolve? How do you change an entire way of conceiving things that people had held on to for as long as they could remember? Do you just announce that one era is over and another has begun? Or do you meet people where they're at, in the language they speak, in the forms they're accustomed to, but then gradually introduce new ideas that help them make changes step by step by step?

So Leviticus is a step?

It was a revolutionary step forward in human consciousness at that time, inviting people to consider a whole new conception of the divine.

Is that what Saint Paul meant when he said the Law (Leviticus et al.) was a tutor?

Yes. A tutor meets you where you're at and helps guide you to the next place. The tutor is necessary for a season, but then you evolve, you grow, you adapt, you gain maturity, only to discover that you no longer need what you once needed.

31

What About
All Those People
Falling Over Dead?

Let's look at a story that we find toward the end of chapter 4 of the book of Acts. It's early in the life of the church, and the writer tells us,

All the believers were one in heart and mind,

and

No one claimed that any of their possessions was their own, but they shared everything they had.

He goes on to write that

from time to time those who owned land or houses sold them, brought the money from the sales and put it at the apostles' feet, and it was distributed to anyone who had need.

Now, enter a man named Ananias, who,

together with his wife Sapphira, also sold a piece of property.

With his wife's knowledge, Ananias keeps part of the money from the sale for himself but then brings the rest of the money to the leaders of the church, pretending that it is *all* of the money he got from the sale.

Peter, one of the leaders of the church, unleashes on him, asking,

Ananias, how is it that Satan has so filled your heart that you have lied to the Holy Spirit and have kept for yourself some of the money you received for the land?

Peter then goes on to ask him more questions, all of it reaching a crescendo with the declaration:

You have not lied just to human beings but to God.

The text then reads:

When Ananias heard this, he fell down and died.

Just like that.

The people who witness this are understandably a bit freaked out (*great fear seized [them],* according to Luke), some young fellas come in and take the body away and bury it, and then three hours later Sapphira shows up. Peter asks her if the money that Ananias had given was the whole sale price of the property, she says yes, Peter asks her how she could test the Holy Spirit, and then he tells her that the fellas who just hauled away her husband's body are right outside and they're ready to carry her out as well.

And then Sapphira falls over dead. Right then and there.
The fellas who carried out her husband's body then carry out her
body, bury her next to her husband, and everybody is freaked out
all over again.

And that's the story.

This story makes me think of the people I've met over the years
who told me that they're starting a new church that's fresh and
real and relevant, you know, *just like the New Testament church.*

Really? Like that one? Like the one in Acts 4 and 5? Because bodies
were dropping right and left in that one . . .
(Please tell me you thought that was funny.)

Now, a few observations about the story.

First, a bit about economics and generosity.
Remember that the writer of this book Acts here has lots of
material to draw from. Lots of stories, lots of accounts, lots of
memories—he has to make choices in writing his account about
what to include and what to leave out. In other words, the ordering
of these stories isn't random. Luke has an agenda, a message, a
distinct story he's telling. And one of the things he wants us to
know at the end of chapter 4 is that

*God's grace was so powerfully at work in them all that there were no
needy persons among them.*

According to Luke, one of the most direct results of the grace of
God at work is people taking care of each other's *material* needs.
Food, water, clothes, shelter, health care, that sort of thing. Grace
to Luke is not an abstract theological concept but a reality that
leads people to take action on behalf of each other.

Grace has implications. Grace leads you somewhere. Grace creates a human connection and community, one grounded in real needs being met by real people in real ways.

Sometimes when people talk about the economy and politics and their convictions about how things should be run, what you subtly (and not so subtly) pick up on is their belief that we're each on our own. It's up to us to figure it out and make our way in the world and work hard to get what we need. It's interesting to note that of all the things Luke could tell us about the early church, one of the most important things he wants us to know is that in the early church, *you weren't on your own.* There were other people looking out for you, others had your back, others would step in and make sure you had what you needed.

Second, let's talk about Peter.
He's a bit harsh, isn't he? Why does he unleash on Ananias and Sapphira like he does? Wasn't the church about grace? They were giving some money, right? Why wasn't he thrilled about that?

Good questions. Let's start with the backstory. Because Peter has a past. He's the one who denied Jesus. This is the dude who, when things got dicey, repeatedly told people that he didn't know Jesus, even though he did know Jesus.

This is *that* dude.

And now he's in charge of the church. Can you see why authenticity is so important to him?

For Peter, it's not about the money. Nowhere in this passage do we see even the slightest shred of greed on the part of the church leaders. What grieves Peter to no end is the dishonesty. *Pretending* is what gets him all fired up.

If you sell your land and keep the money, that's fine. If you sell your land and give the money to the church to distribute to those who need it, that's fine. But whatever you do, according to Peter, don't come in here making a show of your generosity, giving us the impression that this is all the money when it isn't.

Few things will kill the life of a community faster than pretending. (I'm using that word *kill* intentionally.)

It was never about the money, was it? It's about participation. It's about a new kind of world. It's about each of us doing our part, whenever we're able, to contribute to the common good. Sometimes you don't have anything to give. Sometimes you don't have any money, any resources, any hope. And in those moments, you need others. You need to know that you're not on your own.

Which leads us to the people-dying part.

So let's clear up a few things.
First, this is the New Testament, and someone dies. That's how the story goes. Sometimes you'll hear people talk about the Bible like it has two parts: the bloody, violent Old Testament part in which God randomly takes people out for all kinds of reasons, and then the New Testament part in which God suddenly gets nicer because of Jesus and nobody dies.

The truth is, there's a fair bit of death in the New Testament. Have you read the last book in the Bible, Revelation? Lots of death in that one. And there's a ton of love and grace and generosity in the Old Testament. So let's move past those simplistic categories. The Bible is much more complex, because life is much more complex.

Second, then, if you read this story carefully, you'll notice that God is never blamed for the deaths. Ananias and Sapphira fall over dead, but it says nothing about God killing them. Lots of people have asked why God ended their lives, but that's not in the story. The details, as always, matter. (Actually reading whatever it is you're discussing is often quite helpful.)

And then third, when we read this story, we're reading a story written by an actual human being reflecting how he saw the world. Not a new idea but a revolutionary one when reading the Bible. Remember, this story was written in the first century. People had a much more magical and mythical worldview. Volcanoes erupt because the gods are upset, storms come because of conflict between goddesses, and crops don't grow because of divine displeasure. This story was written roughly 1,400 years before the scientific revolution. Data and evidence and proof were not the primary lens through which people saw the world.

Let me put it another way: Let's say you're standing in a jewelry store about to buy your honey a lovely little necklace when a dude runs in wearing a ski mask, waving a gun, yelling, *Nobody move!* You stand there frozen while he empties the display cabinets into a bag, cursing the salespeople for not helping him fast enough, threatening to shoot anyone who moves a muscle. He keeps shouting, *I'm in charge here! You're in my world now! Do as I say!* He then finishes and sprints out the front door into the street . . . where he's hit by a passing garbage truck.

Now. Stop. Pause. Reflect. What are you thinking in that exact second as you watch him get hit? Probably something like

Serves him right.
Or
Well now that's fitting.
Or
He had it coming.

Or
Justice is poetic, isn't it?

If you had any thoughts along those lines, what was happening in
your mind?

You were connecting the two events.

Dude robs a store, gets hit by a truck. The one event led to the
other. Of course. Justice. The universe is put back in balance. *Serves
him right. You reap what you sow. Etc., etc.*

Now, remember that your mind naturally wants to make these
connections even though you've been living in a modern world that
has been under the influence of the scientific revolution for roughly
three hundred years. We've had it drilled into our heads that you
need actual evidence and concrete data to support any sort of
convoluted idea that the two events are connected.

And yet you can't help it.

Now go back two thousand years in history. Can you see how
people living at a much earlier time in human history would
connect the events? Can you see how Luke would tell a story
implying that Ananias and Sapphira's lies led to their deaths?

In the first century, it was very normal and natural to assume that
events, especially unusual or rare events, had supernatural causes.
Luke's storytelling here is an excellent example of how people saw
the world.

We moderns naturally want explanations for what *exactly*
happened. And in the absence of proof and data and explanations,
we create them: maybe they had preexisting heart conditions,

maybe the psychosocial pressures of betraying their community were too much for them to bear, maybe they died later from food poisoning but it was so close to the incident with Peter that Luke couldn't help but write it up more dramatically than it actually happened . . .

We modern folks love to do this. It's like a knee-jerk impulse we immediately default to, taking a story like this and looking for *rational* causes.

All of it missing the power of the story. The farther we go down that rabbit hole, the farther we travel from the power of the story to transform us and wake us up.

Luke wants us to know that the resurrection led to the formation of a community of generous and honest people who gave themselves to the well-being of each other, doing whatever they needed to do to make sure everyone had their needs met. They were highly aware of the divine presence in their midst, leading them and convicting them and giving them hope that a better world really is possible, right here and right now when we all do our part.

Is there a God who struck them down?
Did Peter actually know that they were about to die?
Is this an example of supernatural judgment?

I have no idea.
No one does.

Let the story be what it is.
Let the Bible be what it is.
And then go take care of someone's needs.
And don't pretend you're more righteous than you are.
That'll kill you.

32

Did Jesus Have to Die?

No.
He didn't.
He was killed.

But we're getting ahead of ourselves.

First, a question:

Did you or will you eat a meal today?
Yes, you probably did. And your meal consisted of what? I'm guessing something that was once a plant and maybe something that was once an animal. **In other words, something that was once alive, but in order for you to eat it, it had to die.** The fruit or vegetable had to be harvested, pulled from the soil, picked from a tree. The animal had to be butchered. That's how it works. You have to eat to stay alive, and for you to eat, something has to die.

Your life is dependent on something else's . . . death.

Death is the engine of life. Think about what happens when someone dies doing something heroic, like rescuing someone in trouble or standing up to injustice. We say that their death was *inspiring.* What does it mean to inspire? It means to breathe in life, to give life.

Or take the seasons. In the winter everything dies. And then in the spring it comes back to life. It literally *springs* forth.

Or take your cells. You have many trillion cells in your body right now. They are constantly dying while your body is producing new ones to replace them. Around 300 million cells in your body die and are replaced every *minute*.

Death is the engine of life. All around us, all the time. This death-and-life rhythm is built in to the fabric of creation.

So when you read the Bible and it tells the story of a death that is somehow the engine of new life in the world, *this is not a new story*. This is not a new truth. This is how the world has worked for a long, long time. This idea—this *truth*—did not come out of nowhere.
(Obviously, then, it's not a surprise that stories about death and resurrection have been told in lots of cultures across the ages.)

Which leads us to an observation about the Bible:
The writers of the Bible bear witness to how things are. That's why these stories and images and metaphors and ideas have resonated so deeply with so many people across the ages. Life *is* mysterious. Suffering *does* make you feel like your heart has caved in. Humans *are* capable of astonishingly good and bad acts. People *do* reflect the divine image.

In some traditions that emphasize the importance of the Bible, people can easily pick up the idea that if something is in the Bible, it's true. But it works the other way around: it's in the Bible because the Bible writers were witness to truths larger than any book or tribe or religion.

Which leads us back to the question about why Jesus died.

One response: he was killed.

Betrayed, executed, hung on a cross—Jesus was killed. That's the story we have in the Gospels. You have to start with the actual story, not with all of the theories or systems that you have created. You have to set aside your assumptions about why certain things had to happen or not happen or whatever. You have to let it unfold like an actual story unfolds.

In the story, we're told he came and taught and called disciples and healed and preached and confronted the injustice and indifference of the religious/military/economic machine of his day. It was a violent, unstable, volatile time, and threats to the security of the empire were dealt with swiftly and severely. He was killed.

That's how the story goes. And then, according to the Gospels, he appeared, later, to his disciples. He told them to make students, immersing those disciples in the Trinitarian love of God, and then he was gone.

His followers, of course, struggled to make sense of
what.
just.
happened.

That's how life is: we experience things and then we interpret them, we do our best to explain them, and we look for meaning in them.

We ask, *What does it mean?*

The Bible was written by people. People with perspectives grounded in their cultures and times and places. They're having experiences and undergoing events and then processing and interpreting those events and experiences. That's what the Bible is. It wasn't written by a third party somewhere in the sky who passively and objectively tells you **what the plan is.** It was written by real people in real places at real times doing their best to make sense of it all.

Can you see why questions like *Why did God do it that way?* will never give you satisfying answers? It's the wrong question, which will always result in an unsatisfying answer.

These first Christians interpreted Jesus's life and death through the lens of the sacrificial system because that was one of their primary lenses for understanding God, life, faith, and the events they had experienced.
They believed their God dwelled uniquely in the temple in Jerusalem, the city you went to for offering sacrifices. This was not unusual—throughout the ancient world, temples were understood to be the places where the gods resided, and you went to them to offer tithes and offerings to honor them and keep their favor.

God didn't set up the sacrificial system. People did.
The sacrificial system evolved as humans developed rituals and rites to help them deal with their guilt and fear. (This is why the book of Leviticus is so radical and progressive—in it you can actually know where you stand with God, you can have peace with God, a truly revolutionary idea at the time.) At first, there was the belief that there are forces we are dependent on for our survival. Over time those forces came to be personalized, so it wasn't just the sun—it was the sun god. And then gradually those forces and gods were given names. And personalities. And attributes. And over time this one particular story emerged about *one* God who stood over all the others, who was doing something new in the world.

God didn't need the blood of sacrifices. People did.

This is why the writer of the book of Hebrews keeps talking about how God doesn't need the blood of animals. God never did. We did. Offering sacrifices came out of a deep human need to do something about guilt and shame and the haunting sense that you haven't done enough to keep the gods on your side. It all takes place in an unfolding story.

God didn't need to kill someone to be "happy" with humanity. What kind of God would that be? Awful. Horrific. What the first Christians did was interpret Jesus's death through the lens of the sacrificial system, trusting that the peace humans had been longing for with God for thousands of years was in fact a reality—and always had been—that could be trusted.

Can you see how they would have understood Jesus as the ultimate, last, complete sacrifice?
This is where things get interesting. The story of Jesus dying on the cross as an act of sacrifice is often told and then understood in such a way that it appears primitive and barbaric. And an innocent man being executed is, obviously, extraordinarily primitive and barbaric. But the truth is, the story as we read it is actually *a giant leap forward*. It's a story about humanity growing in maturity, leaving behind the idea that the divine needs blood. That's the giant leap that's happening in the New Testament. The Bible is a reflection of a growing and expanding human consciousness. If you try to freeze it or isolate a particular section or passage as if it exists independent of the time and place in which it was written, you will end up asking the wrong questions. Which will always lead to frustrating and unfulfilling answers.

Jesus was killed. Then his followers insisted that they'd had encounters with him. They reflected on things he said before he died on the cross. They thought about their own history and the central role of the temple in their communal life. They saw in his innocence a picture of the sacrificial lambs they'd all been offering since childhood. They saw in his willingness to die rather than resort to violence a new way to be in the world. They viewed his death as the end of that entire system of bloodshed. And they saw his resurrection as vindication that his way really is a new and better way to be in the world.

We're still finding meaning and significance in his life and death and resurrection. That's why the Bible is referred to as a living and active word. We're still wrestling, still inspired, still questioning, still moved.

33

What About Predestination?

A few years ago, I was speaking somewhere in the Midwest, and at the end of my talk, I took questions, and a young fella stood up with a large Bible open in his hands, and he began his question by reading from the book of Romans, and then he asked me, *Is your God big enough to predestine some people to hell because of divine wrath?*

Or something like that. It was as awkward as it sounds. Part of me at the time considered responding, *So what Bible college do you attend?*

Because it's usually only really, really religious folks who ask questions like that about who is chosen and who isn't and who's elect and who's predestined and who's in and who's out.

So here's what I think about all that: it's a completely ridiculous discussion that only leads to insane debates and ideas that make people miserable and confused, and it distracts them from actually becoming the kind of people Jesus teaches us to be.

There. Settled.

But not really, right? Because why then do we find these words
predestined and *elect* in the Bible? Why did people use these words?
What were they getting at by using these words?

A few thoughts.
First, **election.**
In the scriptures, **election is always instrumental.** What do I
mean by *instrumental*? Think about how we use the word *election*
now: People vote for someone to do a particular task as part of
a particular office (president, student union leader, sanitation
supervisor) by having an election. The person who wins, who's
elected, is elected to do that particular task. People aren't elected
simply to be elected; election is for the purpose of doing something.

Now, let's think about this in relation to the Bible. What is the
Bible about? It's about a tribe of people who have this sense
that they are called to be a tribe unlike the other tribes. At that
time, tribes existed to serve themselves, to accumulate and form
alliances for self-preservation. But this tribe—this tribe starts with
a story about a man named Abram whose God tells him that the
whole world is going to be blessed through him. This tribe believes
they have a calling that extends way beyond themselves, to the
ends of the earth. It's a tribe that exists not just for their own well-
being but also for the well-being of all the other tribes.

Can you see why they may have used a word like *election*? The word
was organically connected with *mission, purpose, calling,* **action** on
behalf of others, for their well-being.

Were they always true to this sense of election?

No. That's what you see in the Gospels again and again: Jesus
calling his tribe back to its origins, to its mission, to its divine
responsibility to be a light to the world.

Second, **predestination.**
The word occurs six times in the Bible.

Six.

In Greek the word is *proorízō,* which is two Greek words: the word
pro, which means *before,*
and
the word *horízō,* from which we get the word *horizon.*
It also means *boundaries* or *limits* or *to mark out beforehand.*

Now, let's look at one verse in Ephesians 1 where it's used. It
says God

predestined us for adoption to sonship through Jesus Christ, in
accordance with [God's] pleasure and will—to the praise of [God's]
glorious grace, which [God] has freely given us in the One [God] loves.

A couple of observations:
The context is adoption.

Have you ever been in an airport and there's a crowd of people
waiting at the gate because a family member or friend of theirs has
gone overseas and adopted a child and now they're about to land
and all these friends and loved ones have gathered to welcome
the family and their new child home? They're holding *welcome*
home signs and they've got stuffed animals and T-shirts that say
grandpa and *grandma* on them. (As if the baby can read! But it's still
moving, isn't it?) And there's always a brother-in-law, the techy one,
who's filming it all. And then the plane lands and the family comes
down the hall and they turn the corner and everybody starts
cheering and crying and hugging and you're standing there totally
caught up in it, aren't you?

Adoption. That's the context of this verse.

In accordance with [God's] pleasure and will . . .

What God does in this verse, namely adopting lots of kids, is for God's pleasure. God is a pleasure seeker, and what brings God immeasurable pleasure is welcoming people home into the family.

Which he has freely given us in the One he loves.

The *One* there is a reference to Jesus. The writer Paul here wants his readers to see the point of Jesus, which is to show us the love that God freely has for all of us, expressed specifically in the love God has for him.

Now, an illustration. Let's say that your friend Lulu from college works in a city far from where you live and you haven't seen her since you graduated, but one day you learn that you're going to be taking a business trip to that city. You track Lulu down and suggest that you get together for a meal while you're in town. You tell her the hotel you'll be staying at, and she emails back that she works just around the corner from there, so why don't you meet her at her work. Sounds great. The day comes and you show up at the address she gave you, which is a little hole-in-the-wall that looks like it used to be a barbershop.

A bit of background on Lulu: She was always organized. Crazy organized. *On it* like no one else. Shelves neatly organized, desk spotless, clothes hung perfectly. Not in a neurotic way, just in a *Wow, Lulu likes things organized* kind of way.

So you walk in the door, and Lulu is sitting at a desk showing something on a large sheet of paper to a woman who is sitting next to her, and they're deep in conversation, and the woman is listening intently to whatever it is Lulu is saying. She sees you and gives you the just-a-minute sign, and so you sit down and watch her. Whatever it is, the woman Lulu is talking to is soaking up her words, and when they're done, the woman thanks Lulu profusely and gives her a hug and says, *I don't know what I'd do without you,* and then walks out.

You and Lulu then greet and hug, and then you ask Lulu the question you are dying to ask, which is, of course,

Lulu, who does your hair?

(Ha-ha-ha-ha-ha, got you! Didn't see that coming, did you?)

No, you don't ask her about her hair, you ask her,

Lulu, what do you do?

She then explains that after college, she got a master's in social work, and then she was hired by city social services, but over time she learned that most of the people she was interacting with needed help organizing their lives, setting up a budget, and prioritizing needs vs. wants, and that if she could help them do that, it might save them lots of hassle and stress in other areas of their lives. So she found this old barbershop and set up a nonprofit life-coaching practice and she's never had more fun.

You are so inspired by this story Lulu is telling, and you think about what she was like in college, and you picture that woman's face who she was helping, and you say,

Lulu, it feels like you were meant to do this.

Now, let's pause and focus on this word *meant* that you just used, because it has huge significance. You're struck with how it seems Lulu was *meant* to do this. What do you mean when you use this word, *meant?* What you mean is: *This isn't an accident. Who Lulu is and the kind of skills she has and the work she's doing aren't random or pointless, but instead, in some very difficult way to describe, it speaks to you about how the universe is supposed to function.*

What you just did in talking about how meaningful it was to watch Lulu do her thing was to refer back in time, to your sense that Lulu's life has been leading up to this moment. To give depth to the power of what she's up to in the present, you placed her job in the context of her whole life, naming the trajectory that you saw early glimpses of in college but are now seeing in its fullness, and it's beautiful. So when the first Christians were trying to explain this extraordinary new thing that was happening in people's hearts and lives through the resurrected Christ, can you see how they used language that implied a sense of intention and purpose from earlier in time?

All that said, a few truths to wrap this up:

People often use words like *elect* and *predestined* to narrow God's actions, but in the Bible they're used to expand our understanding of what God is up to.
The God who freely gives, the God who calls us children because it brings God pleasure, and the people who have a sense of election by which they mean responsibility and destiny to bless others— these words are continually, consciously used to speak of God's expansive desire and efforts to rescue and redeem and restore everything and everybody.

(By the way, if anyone ever quotes Romans chapters 9 to 11 while arguing their case for why some are predestined and some aren't, point out to them that the crescendo of that particular section is 11:26, where Paul writes that all Israel will be saved.

All. Israel. Will. Be. Saved.

If the passage is about some kind of God who chooses some and not others, then why is the exclamation point at the end in the form of the message that all of Israel will be saved?)

When you come across something that religious people have been debating and discussing for years, always ask yourself, *What would happen if I actually had concrete answers to the questions?*
When I have been asked whether some are chosen or not, I always ask, *How would you ever know such a thing?* and more importantly, *How would that ever make your life better?*

Some things that religious people make a big deal of are rather pointless. Avoid the insanity.

How often do you ask, *What would it feel like to swallow a hair dryer while it was turned on?*

No, you don't, because it's not interesting. And if you could answer the question, what would you gain?

Oh, and that guy who stood up and asked that question?
My answer was:

No.

34

What About All That Wrath?

Let's read a bit from the letter to the Romans:

What if God, although choosing to show [God's] wrath and make [God's] power known, bore with great patience the objects of [God's] wrath—prepared for destruction?

Yep. That's a strange passage on first read. And of course there's something bigger going on in that chapter than what appears on first reading.

First, chapters 9 to 11 in the letter to the Romans are a bit like an extended riff. So you need to read them as a continuous thought. It's like the writer Paul pauses at the end of chapter 8 because he knows that what he's written so far to his friends in Rome will raise some questions, and so he takes a minute to anticipate their questions in 9 through 11, and then he picks back up in chapter 12.

Second, how does chapter 11 begin? With a question. And what is the question?

Did God reject [God's] people? By no means!

Interesting, isn't it? Because often people read chapter 9 and the bits about wrath and say, *See? Some people are objects of wrath, destined for the trash heap! They've rejected God and they're gonna burn!*

But if you keep reading, that's exactly the thing that Paul insists he *isn't* saying.
He talks about their

full inclusion (his words, not mine).

Then he writes that the gifts and calling of God are *irrevocable,*

and then he writes that God does what God does

so that [God] may have mercy on them all.

And, oh yes, he also mentions in chapter 11 that

all Israel will be saved.

(That's chapter 11, verse 26.)

They will?
What do you do with that?

Full inclusion,
irrevocable,
have mercy on them all,
all saved.

Those are the actual words used in this passage. So when someone starts talking about wrath and all that, it's important that they also talk about inclusion and mercy.

Can you see how easy it is to grab a few words from the Bible and make it say pretty much whatever you want it to?

The writer Paul is painting a picture of a loving and merciful divine being who invites you to *trust*. Love, grace, power, salvation—you're invited to trust that God is really that good. That love really is the ground of our being. That everybody ultimately resides in the goodness of this God. That everything you could ever try to do to get in good with this God has already been done.

Can you resist this goodness? Of course you can—people do it all the time. Can you choose isolation and violence and negativity and cynicism? Of course you can—people do it all the time. Can you allow your heart to grow cold and your life to become self-centered, manufacturing your own hell on earth right here, right now? Of course—people do it all the time.

But if a person chooses that path, it's their choice, not God's. God is love, grace, mercy—inviting all of us to trust that that kind of life is actually possible right here, right now.

Now, one more thought: Is it satire?
Is Paul actually using this over-the-top imagery to make his point? Notice in chapter 9 where he writes,

You will say to me . . .

He's clearly conducting an imaginary (I couldn't think of a better word) conversation with his readers. They have strict categories they've been raised with for who's in and who's out. That's how they see the world. And of course in their thinking, they're *in*. (The people who talk like this are always *in* according to their own estimation, aren't they?)

Is this actually a bit of brilliant, subversive writing, where he takes the position of his friends who would object to his bigger point, spoofing their perspective, in order to then paint a picture so much bigger and truer and more loving and more beautiful than anything they could imagine that it blows their minds?

Is this passage actually way more inclusive and clever and expansive and transcendent than most people who read it realize? Is this passage that is often used to justify the belief that God intends to send billions of people to burn in hell and be tortured forever actually a passage about the grace and mercy of the God who wants everybody included and thriving and saved from whatever they need saving from?

And then one more point to add to my one more point: How does chapter 11 end?

With a hymn of euphoric praise.

Literally, it reads,

For from [God] and through [God] and for [God] are all things.

Does that sound like the kind of God who discards people? Does that sound like a divine being who casts actual human beings onto a trash heap? The passage ends with an exultant declaration of the unity of this God, of the power of this God who holds all things and people and events together. Whole. Healed. Connected. One.

Where's the wrath in that?

35

What About Sin?

Let me see if I can clear a few things up in less than a thousand words.

First, if I were to ask you to define the word *sin,* how would you answer?

My guess is you'd probably say something like *Sin is when you break God's laws* or *Sin is disobeying God* or *Sin is whatever you do that makes God angry.*

While those may sound accurate, they don't tell the whole story. Which is why many don't know what to do with the word other than cringe when people use it with a straight face.

Now, for a definition. The theologian Cornelius Plantinga Jr. in his book *Engaging God's World* puts it like this:

Sin is culpable disturbance of shalom.

Shalom. *Shalom* is the Hebrew word for *peace, wholeness, health,* and *blessing.* Shalom is the harmony God intends for the world.

Shalom is how God wants things to be. Shalom is peace with yourself, with your neighbor, with the earth, with God.

Disturbance. Things aren't how they're supposed to be, are they? From environmental degradation to domestic violence to Wall Street corruption to the petty little ways we disrespect each other, this world isn't everything it could be.

Culpable. Guilt, responsibility, ownership—culpable is any way you have contributed to the disturbance of shalom we see all around us.

Sin is anything we do to disrupt the peace and harmony God desires for the world.

Here's the problem with how many understand the word: When sin is understood primarily in terms of *breaking* or *violating* or *disobeying,* there's no larger context to place it in. There's whatever you did or didn't do, and then there's God's anger or wrath or displeasure with you.

But when you place it in the larger context of the good, the peace, the shalom that we all want for the world, then it starts to make way more sense. Of course I'm guilty of disturbing shalom. *Is there any sane person who wouldn't own up to that?*

In the Bible, we are not primarily identified as sinners, but as saints. This is important: your primary identity, your true self, is found in who you are in Christ, not in the ways you have disrupted shalom.

In the Bible, people are taught first who they are, because the more you know about who you are, the more you'll know what to do.

This is why some sermons that talk a lot about Jesus can be so soul sucking. They aren't an announcement about who you are in Christ—they're all about what you're not. They're boring and lifeless and produce all kinds of despair even though they quote lots of Bible verses because they mistakenly teach you that your identity is found in your sin. It's not. It's found in Christ, who has taken care of your sins.

In the Bible, there's only one kind of sin—the kind that God has forgiven in Christ. There's no other kind. And so we do what we can to make amends with whoever we've sinned against, trusting that the only kind of sin there is, is forgiven sin.
In the Bible, sin is the middle word about you. The first word is that you're created in the image of God, crowned with glory and honor, a child of the divine. That's who you are.
The second word is the honest, unvarnished truth about how we all fall short. We all sin; we all disrupt the shalom that God intends for all things.
The third word is the continual insistence that the last word hasn't been spoken about you and your sin, that all sins have been forgiven in Christ, that we are loved and restored, redeemed, reconciled, and renewed. That's what the writers return to again and again and again.

One more truth about this word *sin*.

A question: What is rape?

If I told you that rape is something that is not nice, how would you respond?
Or if I told you that it's really helpful when people rape less, what would you say?

Or if I told you that rape just isn't the best thing that a person can do . . .

Please tell me you're crawling out of your skin right about now. Why? Because I didn't use words that are strong enough and adequate enough to describe just how evil and horrific rape is.

Some words are strong for a reason. We need them to describe realities that demand that kind of strong language. *Sin* is one of those words. Let's keep it.

36

Is It the Word of God?

To begin with, a few words about words.

Sometime around 1993 I was studying to be a pastor, and I took a class in preaching from Rev. Dr. Mitties McDonald DeChamplain. She's a legend, and it was a thrill to learn from her. I was just starting out, but I had big ideas about preaching and how it could be done in new ways, and I threw myself into the craft, trying to learn everything I could while getting as much experience as I could. As part of my time studying with her, I got to give a short sermon to the class. I had learned early on in seminary that there was a way seminary folks approached sermons and that I didn't see it that way—I was after something else. Something different. Something new. So I worked and worked to prepare my sermon, trying to get it how I thought it should be.

And then the day came, and I gave that sermon. I can only imagine how rough it must have been for my fellow students, but I was on top of the world. I felt like I'd tapped into something, like I was finding my voice, like the sky was the limit with what would be done with this particular art form called the sermon.

I sat down, and it was time for the class to comment. They were kind and supportive and said what you say when you know this same person you're evaluating is going to evaluate you later. Polite, in other words.

And then it was Dr. DeChamplain's turn to give me feedback. You know what she said?

You can take it way farther.

That's what she said. She didn't wonder why I did it the way I did it, she didn't tell me how to do it better, and she didn't give me a list of things to work on. She somehow understood what I was up to, and she let me know she was behind me and I should keep going and there was no limit.

You can take it way farther.

Words have power. Twenty-five years later her words are still with me.

There are those moments when someone says exactly what you need to hear—you know there's more, you know that what you've been taught wasn't the last word on the matter, and you have a sense that you were missing something, and then you hear someone say it. They name it, call it out, describe it, *insist it is possible,* give it language—whatever it is that they say, it makes your heart leap.

Or maybe you were in a bad place. Filled with despair and doubt, wondering if there was any way forward, and someone said something that changed everything. It inspired you, moved you, spurred you to action, gave you hope that there was a way forward.

Words can do that.

Words . . . can create new worlds. (Heschel said that.)
Words can change everything.

So when you open the Bible and start reading the poem on the first page, does it surprise you that the poet describes a God who creates using . . . *words?*

Words create new realities. And when this God speaks, the poet insists, things happen.

The word for *word* and *to speak* in Hebrew is *davar,* and it's used around 1,400 times in the Bible. God speaks, God *davar*s, and things happen. The word for *word* is also the word for *thing* and *power*—something written, spoken, heard, seen, and experienced. **A creative act that brings something new into existence.**

The writers of the Bible believed that this life has a source, that it flows from the heart of a divine being who is good and creative and generous and on our side. As Paul asked a crowd of people in the city of Lystra,

Who do you think it is that provides your food and fills you with joy?

According to the Hebrews, there is a creative life force that surges through all creation, giving it life and sustaining it, from the movement of the planets to the breath of a child. God speaks, and then God continues to speak. As the Psalm writer puts it, God continually works to

renew the face of the ground.

In the Bible, the whole universe is God's megaphone.

God speaks, God acts, God creates, God sustains—God is the source of the endless energy that pours forth into creation, bringing new life and sustaining everything from trees and rocks to hearts and minds.

So the Bible is the word of God?
Yes. Lots of things are.

Wait—lots of things are the word of God?
That's what you find in the Bible—
from the heavens and the stars (the Psalms)
to
the mouth of a baby (again, the Psalms)
to
your conscience (Romans)
to
the poets and philosophers of the day (Paul quotes a number of them in Acts 17).

So when you read the word of God, you find the writers of the word of God talking about lots of words of God?
Yes. Remember, the Bible was written over a thousand years before the printing press. People didn't have their own copy of the Bible. At best your village may have had a scroll in the synagogue. One, for the whole village. And before that, very little was written down. These stories circulated as oral history, passed down from one generation to the next. So when the writers referred to the word of God, they weren't talking about a book or a library of books as we think of them. They were talking about something much bigger than that.

So how would you define the word of God?
The creative action of God speaking in and through the world, bringing new creation and new life into being.

So what do people mean when they say that this library of books written by people is the word of God?

What they're saying is that they find this library of books to be a reliable record of what the ongoing, unfolding creative work of God looks like in the world.

But can't you experience that through lots of books, lots of other words, lots of other experiences?
Of course. That's something the writers of the Bible say often. It's as if the writers keep saying, *Open your eyes, look around, listen, and pay attention. God is always speaking—the whole thing is a word.*

So one of the main points of the library of books that some refer to as the word of God is that there are lots of words of God and you can and should listen to them all?
Exactly.

37

Is It Authoritative?

There are verses about *God* having authority and verses about Jesus, governments, prophets, kings, soldiers, masters, and leaders having authority, but as far as the *Bible* having authority, that's not the exact language that we find in the Bible. What we find is something much more interesting.

Let's spend a moment on this word *authority*. To do so, we'll look at a passage in the apostle Paul's letter to the Corinthians, where he tells them about

the authority the Lord gave me for building you up, not for tearing you down.

The word for *authority* Paul uses here is the Greek word *exousia*— which is made up of two words:
ek, which means *out from,*
and
eimi, which is the verb *to be.*

The word is generally translated as *weight, power, influence,* and, of course, *authority.* It's an active word, referring to the power to act in particular ways for particular purposes. It's something you have, but you have it in the dynamic sense of doing something with it. (It's also a feminine word.)

Now, let's think about *exousia* in terms of the Bible.

First, the Bible has to be interpreted.
When someone says they're *just doing what the Bible says to do,* they didn't greet you with a holy kiss, they're probably wearing two kinds of fabric sewn together, and there's a good chance they don't have tassels sewn on the corners of their garments, all things commanded in the Bible. They don't do those things because they don't believe those commands are binding on them today. **And they don't believe that or practice those things because they've interpreted the Bible in a particular way.** Or more likely, they've been influenced by someone who told them that is how the Bible is to be interpreted.

Someone who they have given authority to. They have given that parent, teacher, pastor, priest, youth leader—whoever—*authority* over them. Weight, power, influence.

Some people have authority over you because of circumstance— like police and government leaders and the IRS. Other people have authority because you give them authority.

The roof on our house used to leak. When it rained—which in California actually happened once, I just can't remember it, ha-ha—we literally had to put out buckets in the kitchen because of how much water came through the cracks. So we called the roof company and they came out and the guy inspected things and did some repairs and then asked me to come up on the roof to show me what he'd done and what still needed to be done. The guy is an expert, and when he's showing me how to fix our roof, I give him *exousia*—I give him weight and influence and authority because I want the roof to stop leaking.

Really basic but important when you're asking questions about the authority of the Bible.

Second, then, it's important to understand that authority is a relational reality. Here's what I mean: When people talk about the authority of the Bible, what they're generally referring to is the need for you to do what it says—to obey, to believe, and to submit to it. The Bible in that context is often described as the objective, absolute truth of God, and so the only proper response is to follow it.

But following it, obeying it, submitting to it—whatever language you want to use—cannot be done without interpretation. And interpretation requires actual people to do the interpreting. Someone has to decide what the Bible says, what it means, and what that looks like in flesh and blood.

This is why so many people are so confused when it comes to the Bible. They were taught by their pastor or parents or authority figures to submit to the authority of the Bible, but **that's impossible to do without submitting first to whoever is deciding what the Bible is even saying.** And that requires trust. Because authority is a relational reality. Someone told you, *This is how it is.* The problem, of course, is that the folks who talk the most about the authority of the Bible also seem to talk the most about things like objective and absolute truth, truth that exists *independent of relational realities.*

What often happens, then, is people grow up or start reading or travel or go to university or make friends outside of their tribe, and in the process, they discover that things *aren't how they were told things are.*

They realize that what they were told is *simply how it is* in an absolute and objective way, is actually a set of interpretations made by actual humans. Humans who have a limited perspective.

And what it feels like is betrayal.
Like you were sold a bill of goods.

Whenever I meet angry or bruised former religious folks who talk about being *burned by the church* or *disillusioned with Christianity* or *done with the Bible,* I always ask questions about their past, about who they trusted and what happened, because these issues of authority are relational realities.

So what is authority again?
Authority is when you give weight, power, and influence to something.

So we can give weight and power and influence to this ancient library of books with our minds and hearts fully awake and engaged?
Absolutely. That's the only way to give it authority.

And that doesn't mean we blindly accept it—it means we think about it and interpret it and wrestle with it and discuss it and challenge it?
Yes.

38

What About the Contradictions?

Again the anger of the LORD burned against Israel, and he incited David against them, saying, "Go and take a census of Israel and Judah."

—2 Samuel 24

Satan rose up against Israel and incited David to take a census.

—1 Chronicles 21

So which is it?

Did the Lord incite David to take a census,
or
did Satan incite David to take a census?

The one scripture says one thing, and the other scripture says something else, something completely different.

What do we do with a contradiction like this?

Several things.

First, a bit about why a census is a big deal. You take a census because you want to know how many people you have in your kingdom. And why would you want to know that? Because the more people you have, the more money in taxes you can bring in. And the more money you bring in, the bigger you can build your army. And the size of your army determines who you can go to war against and who you can't. Taking a census, then, is how you know in very practical ways how big you can build your empire.

Why is this a big deal at this point in the Bible? Because—as we've seen again and again—this library of books is about a new kind of tribe in the world. A tribe with a calling, a destiny to be different. A tribe that has a mission to bless all the other tribes. And again and again, this tribe is invited to trust that their God will take care of them.

To take a census, then, is to play the same old game all the other tribes are playing, the empire-building, going-to-war game, keeping violence and destruction in circulation.

Do you see how the census is a deeply spiritual issue—can these people trust that there's a new and better way to be a tribe?

Second, on to the contradiction part.

The 2 Samuel account of this census was written sometime around 600 to 500 BC.

The 1 Chronicles account was written around 400 to 250 BC.

So the 2 Samuel passage was written *earlier—several hundred years* earlier.

The earlier account is the one that said that God led David to do something bad, and the later account says that Satan led him to do it.

Why is this interesting?
Because in the earlier account, God does the inciting.

And why is that interesting?
Because in the ancient world, people often attributed all sorts of anger and violence to their gods because that's how people conceived of the gods. They believed that the gods were mean and vindictive and you needed to sacrifice to them and give offerings to them to appease their anger and keep them on your side.

And how does that explain these two conflicting accounts?
Over time, people evolved in their thinking about God. At a point in history, the idea emerged that a *good* God wouldn't incite someone to do something *bad,* so there must have been some other force leading and inciting David.

And that's where the Satan explanation came in?
Yes. You can see how the idea of an opposing, evil, destructive force/spirit/god/goddess emerged as people became more sophisticated in their thinking.

But what about the Garden of Eden?
It doesn't say anywhere in that story that it's Satan—it says it's a talking snake.

But people often say that it was Satan tempting them in the garden.
They do often say that.

But it doesn't actually say that in the Bible?
It doesn't. And talking snakes were a common literary device in stories from around that time in history.

So when does the word *Satan* first occur in the Bible?
In this passage right here, 1 Chronicles 21.

Really—not until 1 Chronicles?
Yes—and Chronicles wasn't written until the exile, much later in the history of Israel.

So the idea of Satan doesn't emerge until late in the Bible?
Yes.

And what does the word mean?
It's literally *ha satan* in Hebrew. It means *the accuser*.

So it's not really a name at all, more like a title?
Exactly.

And the idea of Satan didn't emerge until the exile, until the Hebrews had experienced extraordinary evil and oppression and had found themselves in a foreign land miles from home in the midst of great alienation and suffering?
Yes.

So there isn't a contradiction between these two passages, more like an evolution?
That's a great word for it. From the earlier passage to the later passage, we see a growing sophistication in how people conceived

of God and evil. They're learning that this God is a new kind of God, different than the other gods, *a God who doesn't do evil or incite people to do wrong,* and their language is reflecting that. By the later passage, a distinction is made that the people living hundreds of years earlier wouldn't have made.

Are there other places within the Bible that reflect growing and shifting thinking?
Yes. In fact, the whole library. That's the point.

39

Is It Inerrant?

To answer the question,
Is the Bible inerrant, or without error?

Let's start with a few questions about Mozart:

Did Mozart's symphonies win?
In your estimation, has Mozart prevailed?
Do Mozart's songs take the cake?
Are his concertos true?

Odd questions, right?
They're odd because that's not how you think of Mozart's music.
They're the wrong categories.

What you do with Mozart's music is you listen to it and you experience it and maybe you study it or play it but mostly you enjoy it.

That's the problem with the word *inerrant* when it comes to the Bible: it's the wrong category.

First, *inerrant* isn't a word that is used anywhere in the Bible to refer to the Bible.
The writers talk about the word of God and inspiration and authority and God breathing because they had lots of ways of getting at the truth of the scriptures.

Second, the writers of the Bible were doing something far more significant than trying to write letters and books and tell stories without errors. To describe the Bible as inerrant, then, is to use a word that actually minimizes the importance of what these writers were up to.

What the writers of the Bible do talk about is events unfolding in actual human history they believed reveal a God who is up to something in the world. What they're interested in is their readers seeing this movement and joining it and finding life in it. To describe this movement, they use images and symbols and parables and visions and dreams and prayers and historical accounts and hints and just about every kind of writing imaginable.

It's important then, not to cram the Bible into categories that the Bible itself doesn't acknowledge.
What we have is a library of books written by a number of people over a long period of time. Sometimes they're *for* divorce; sometimes they're *against it*. One says Jesus was from Nazareth, another from Bethlehem. One says David paid *X* for a piece of land, another says he paid *Y*.

The list is long.

Sometimes the writer has an agenda and is working in a particular style and referencing current events in such a way that we in modern times simply can't get at what exactly is going on in what they wrote.

Sometimes it's a poem,
other times it's a parable,
and sometimes things are exaggerated because the writer is making
a much larger point.

Other times we have assumptions about history and how it's
recorded that aren't shared by the writer, and so we're reading it
trying to figure out how they got it so wrong when they weren't
writing with that particular intention in the first place.

It was believed that Emperor Caesar, at the end of his life,
ascended to the heavens to sit at the right hand of the gods—is
that why Luke ends his book with Jesus ascending? Where did Jesus
go? Up into the sky? Because we've sent spaceships up there, and
no one saw him. We assume Luke is writing the actual details of
what happened, but when you back up and realize that Luke wants
his audience to see *Jesus* as Lord, not Caesar, then the way he
describes Jesus ascending starts to make more sense. We moderns
love history to be precise with times and dates and actual facts.
That's why we're still fascinated with the JFK assassination—it feels
like we don't have all of the exact facts. But ancient writers had
different agendas. Luke isn't trying to mislead—he's telling a story
in the way people in his day told stories.

However you deal with the funkiness (I couldn't think of a better
word) of the Bible, if you deny it or avoid it or act like it's easily
dismissible, you'll miss something central to the power and life of
the Bible.

**The power of the Bible comes not from avoiding what it is but by
embracing what it is.**

**To argue for inerrancy is arguing for a different kind of library of
books, a library that we don't have.**

We weren't given a science textbook.
Or an owner's manual.
Or a hermeneutically sealed document.

What we have is a fascinating, messy, unpredictable, sometimes breathtakingly beautiful, other times viscerally repulsive collection of stories and poems and letters and accounts and Gospels that reflect the growing conviction that we matter, that everything is connected, and that human history is headed somewhere.

To fully appreciate the Bible, you have to let it be what it is.

Which leads me to one last question: **If something extraordinary and real and compelling was happening in human history, how else would it have been written down?**

Or to put it another way: **When it comes to the Bible, what were you expecting?**

Or to put it another way: Where did people get the idea that *without error* is the highest form of truth?

Is the sunset without error?
Is the love between you and the person you're in love with without error?
Is the best meal you've ever eaten without error?
You don't think about those experiences in those terms because that would rob those experiences of their depth and joy.

So when you are trying to talk about those experiences, you need poems and images and pictures and stories—which of course is what we find in the Bible.

So is the Bible inerrant?
I have a higher view of the Bible than that.

40

Is It Inspired?

All Scripture is theopneustos and is useful for
teaching, rebuking, correcting and training . . .

—2 Timothy 3

Second Timothy, chapter 3, verse 16 uses that word: *theopneustos*.

This word *theopneustos* is a rare one, found nowhere else in the
Bible but this verse.

It's actually two Greek words attached to each other—
the word *theos,* which means *God,*
and
the word *pneó,* which refers to *breathing.*

Scripture, according to the apostle Paul here, is

God-breathed.

First, then, a bit about this word *pneó,*
then a bit about what it means to be God-breathed,
and then third, what this has to do with the Bible.

Pneó.
You'll find this Greek word lurking in a number of English words
having to do with breathing, like *pneumonia,* an illness related
to breathing, and *pneumatic. Pneó* is related to the Greek word
pneuma, which means breath and also . . .

spirit.

You'll find this dual meaning in lots of languages, from Hebrew
(*ruach*) to Latin (*spire*)—the word for *breath* being the same word as
the word for *spirit.*
To *ex*pire is what happens when the life of something leaves it; to
be *in*spired is to have been *breathed into.*

We're all breathed into.

In the opening chapters of the book of Genesis, there's a beautiful
picture of God taking the dust of the ground and breathing into it
the breath of life.

Which leads us to you.

You are made of skin and bones and blood and hair and brain
cells. These different parts of you comprise your physicality, your
body—your tangible, material essence.

And yet that's not all that makes you, you.

You also have a spirit, a soul, consciousness, thoughts . . .

**There is the tangible dimension to your existence—
skin and bones and wood and rocks and dirt and light—**

**and then there is the intangible dimension to your existence—
love and hope and spirit and longing.**

Life is a blend of the two.

Without spirit, you only have physical, lifeless elements; without the physical and material, you only have disembodied ideas. What is love without the embrace of another? What is hope without an actual heart that fills with hope in space and time?

If you've ever been in a room with someone who is about to die, you know exactly what I'm talking about. The person is there, their body lying on the bed, their breath labored and slow, and yet you can sense that something is leaving them. Something you can't see, can't touch, can't measure in a lab, and yet it's something vital and essential to them being *alive*.

Can you see why in so many languages the word for *spirit* and *breath* is the same?

From early on we humans have had the awareness that your breath is intimately tied in to your existence. You stop breathing, you die. Your breath is both a physical reality that can be measured and detected and also a picture of an unseen reality that animates and sustains your existence at the deepest levels of your being.

If you're alive, you're breathing.
You've also been breathed into by the divine.

When we talk about the spirit of something, then, what we're naming is the reality of whatever it is that transcends its physicality. People talk about the spirit of a place, a team, a home, a person—we often refer to the quality and character of something in ways that can't be measured by any tangible means.

Take a song, for example. Certain pieces of music move us in unique and powerful ways, and the word we often use is *inspiring*. What do we mean by this? We mean that the song is chords and notes and sounds and harmony and volume and all those physical, tangible elements, and yet there is something else to the song, something beyond its material essence, that speaks to us.

It breathed into you something good, hopeful, true, comforting, healing, or genuine.

So when Paul writes that the scriptures (which, for an observant Jewish man like Paul would have been the Torah, the prophets, and the wisdom writings) are God-breathed, he's saying that they're books, but they're more than books. They're useful (the word he uses is *óphelimos,* which also translates as *profitable* or *beneficial*) for a number of things that help us do good in the world.

That's actually what he says. That God uses these writings to help you do good in the world. (When a man like Paul talked about doing good, he was referring to the *mitzvot,* which are good deeds that help repair and restore the world.)

How does that work?
In a number of ways.

First, what we find in the Bible is the consistent affirmation that life is a good, precious, sacred gift from God.

It's easy to become numb, bitter, cynical, and jaded, rolling your eyes a lot, checking out, mailing it in, taking each breath you're given for granted. The Bible is a book about remembering, about being awake, about practicing gratitude, about having your eyes open.

Second, what you find in the Bible is the consistent affirmation that how you respond to this gift is of utmost importance.

There are lots of reasons all around us every day to make us believe that we don't matter, that our choices aren't significant, that it's all just a meaningless slide into nothingness. The writers of the Bible speak against this, insisting that you can make choices to live in particular ways, that you can decide to use your voice and your energies for healing and building up, and that you can help take things in a different direction. In story after story, the hero is flawed and frail, prone to make all kinds of mistakes, stumbling through life with a fairly pathetic batting average. In other words, the Bible is a library of books about people a lot like us, trying to figure it out, doing what they can to make a go of it.

So, then, the Bible is inspired in much the same way that you are inspired.
You're just a humble, stumbling bag of bones and skin, and yet the divine, infinite, eternal creative force of the universe has breathed into you. The Bible is a library of books, written by people trying to figure it out, wrestling with their demons, doubting, struggling, doing what they could to bring a little light to their world, and yet these books have been breathed into, showing us what redemption looks like, giving us hope, insisting that people like you and me can actually do our part to heal, repair, and restore this world we call home.

And that is inspiring.

41

What's the Best Question to Ask When You're Reading the Bible?

Why did people find this important to write down?

Start there.
There are lots of other questions you can ask, and many of them can be very illuminating, but start with this one.
Why did people feel the need to write about this?

For example, the first chapter of the Bible, Genesis 1. When was Genesis edited together? When the Israelites found themselves in exile in Babylon. The Babylonians had a creation story called the Enuma Elish. In the Enuma Elish, the god Marduk defeated the goddess Tiamat and then tore her carcass apart, using the two halves to make the world.

Fairly violent, isn't it?

Creation stories were incredibly important in the ancient world (and now) because they rooted and grounded you in a particular view of who you are and what you're doing here. And at the heart of the Babylonian story was an understanding that violence is the engine of creation. That's how the world was created. That's how we got here.

The Israelites were conquered by the Babylonians and hauled away from their homeland to the foreign world of Babylon where they're trying to maintain their sense of identity and tribe, surrounded by the dominant culture and stories of Babylon.

And what do they do in exile? They begin to compile the Hebrew scriptures, which begin with *their* tribe's creation story. Which is a poem. A poem in which beauty and diversity and difference and order are celebrated. A poem in which the engine of creation is divine joy.

Not destruction—overflowing generosity.
Not violence—joy.

Can you see why they found power and meaning in the Genesis 1 poem? It offered a competing creation story to the Babylonian creation story. It confronted the dominant thinking of the world they found themselves in with a different, better vision of what it means to be human.

There's more. These were people miles from home, longing to be freed from their exile. Can you see why they would have found great comfort and hope in the Exodus story, which was about a time long before then when their ancestors were miles from home, longing to be freed?

People wrote and compiled and edited these stories and texts and scriptures because they spoke directly to their deepest questions about life.

Like in the Gospels.
The Romans had conquered Israel, which created a deep sense of shame.

If our God is the God of the world, why has a nation that doesn't even acknowledge our God conquered us?

Can you see how this question would have lingered in the air?

How would you, week after week, go to synagogue and chant a prayer or psalm about the goodness of your God when there were Roman soldiers marching thousands at a time (called a legion) through your land, completely disregarding your God?

So when Jesus asks a demon-possessed man his name and the man says *Legion,* you see what's going on here? Jesus casts the demons out, but the power of the story is Jesus casting out the shame, calling his people back to their destiny.

People wrote these stories down because they *found in them something that* helped restore their dignity; the stories gave them a sense of identity; they helped give voice to their pain.

Like the letters to the Corinthians in the New Testament.
The apostle Paul is stoking a movement, spreading this intoxicating message that there's another way to be in the world, that the good news of Jesus is about human dignity and goodness. He even uses the phrase *new humanity*. And the people he's interacting with are

stuck in all sorts of old, destructive modes of being. They're not getting it as quickly as he'd like. And he's frustrated, but he loves them and he's full of hope but at his wit's end. He cares deeply, and they're also driving him crazy. He's suffering for his work, but it's also doing something profound in him.

He's having to address really practical matters like food and who's sleeping with who and hair and marriage, and then he's also writing things like

Love is patient, love is kind.

He's all over the place.

Why did he write all this in a letter? Because he's got a giant heart for these people, and he wants them to see what he's seen so they'll be filled with the same joy he's being filled with.

———————

Why did people write this down?
What was going on in their world that this was important to them?
Why did they feel the need to put words to this?

Start with that question.
Start with those questions.
And see what happens.

42

What's the Worst Question to Ask When You're Reading the Bible?

It's a question that begins with these three words:

Why did God . . . ?

I'm assuming you've heard some version of this question—or asked it yourself—something like

Why did God tell those people to kill those other people?
or
Why would God create people if God knew they would screw things up?
or
Why couldn't God have just skipped the sacrificial system?
or
Why did Jesus have to die—couldn't God have saved the world some other way?

or

Why does God make it so hard to believe in God?

You've heard these, right?

The problem with questions like these is that they have a world of assumptions built into them, assumptions about God and the Bible that will never get you to a satisfying answer.

Here's what I mean: if you were to ask the person asking the question where they got their ideas about this being named *God* that they have questions about, they would most likely reply, *From the Bible.*

Are you with me here?
Do you see why this can be a problem?

The person asking questions like these already has a number of assumptions and beliefs and thoughts about God and the Bible that they bring to their reading of the Bible. **So while they're reading it, they're constantly comparing what they're reading to what they have already decided about who God is and what God is like.** (This is especially true of religious folks who grew up hearing about a particular version of God—it can be very, very difficult to read the Bible any other way.)

Let's start with an exercise: You have thoughts about God and the Bible. Beliefs. Skepticism. Convictions. Frustration. Experiences. Things people have told you. Things you've read. Opinions about the God you do or don't believe in. Whatever else. Imagine those thoughts as marbles. Each one a shiny little ball.

Got it? Good. Now, take all those marbles and put them in your pocket. Or in a bucket. Or in the cup holder in your car. You get the point. Set them aside. Put them out of sight.

Now, read the Bible.
Without any of those marbles.

Go ahead.
Try it.
Pick a random passage.
Jump in.
Do your best to read it without any ideas about God entering
the picture.

If you do this, all you have is the words on the page. Written by
people, passed down by people, edited by people, decided on
by people.

That's what you have.

So when you read that

God told them to kill everyone in the village,

someone wrote that.
That's how someone understood that event.
Don't drag God into it.

The Bible is a library of books reflecting how human beings have
understood the divine.

People at that time believed the gods were with them when they
went to war and killed everyone in the village.

What you're reading is someone's perspective that reflects the
time and the place they lived in.

It's not God's perspective—
it's theirs.

And when they say it's God's perspective,
what they're telling you is their perspective on God's perspective.

Don't confuse the two.

The art, the challenge, the invitation in reading the Bible, then, is to be as aware as you can of your marbles and keep them in the drawer as long as you can. This is often why people who grew up in church go away to college and take a class in literature or comparative religions and have to read the Bible as part of their coursework and suddenly find it fascinating. Their upbringing actually inoculated them against the compelling nature of the Bible because it spent too much time telling them what it is.

Beware of sermons in which the point is to prove something about the Bible.

The Bible is not an argument. It is a record of human experience. The point is not to prove that it's the word of God or it's inspired or it's whatever the current word is that people are using. The point is to enter into its stories with such intention and vitality that you find what it is that inspired people to write these books.

(When you find something inspiring, the last thing on your mind is proving that it's inspired—you're too caught up in actually being inspired.)

If you're trying to prove what it is,
you're already lost in the deep weeds.

You have to let it be what it is.
There are lots of passages that are quite mysterious, words in the original language we don't have adequate modern equivalents for, and stories that involve practices and rituals we don't have any context for.

But if you keep your marbles in the bucket, and you read and listen carefully, you start to see the story behind the story, **the story about people waking up to bigger and more expansive understandings of who they understand God to be and what they believe God is up to in the world.**

Your questions, then, start to take on a new character, because you begin to realize that the more you enter into the humanity of their story, the more you discover that there's something at work, something insistent, something enduring, something that won't let these people go.

And then you realize that that same force, presence, pull, and call are at work today within you. And in those around you.
And whatever it is that won't let those people go, won't let you go.

43

What's the Other Best Question to Ask When You're Reading the Bible?

So the best question,
the one you start with when you're reading the Bible,
is,
Why did people write this down in the first place?

And then the other best question to ask is,

Why did this passage endure?

Or
Why is it still around, thousands of years later?
Why did people protect and preserve it?
Why have people literally risked their lives to reproduce and distribute
this library of books?

And those questions will always lead you to even better questions.

Why has this story/passage/verse/account resonated with people for this long?
What does this teach us about what it means to be alive, here, in this world, now?

And that question will lead you to this one:

What is it that was true about this book or story or poem or letter for them at that time that's also true for us, here and now?

For example, the Psalms.
From Psalm 13:
How long, LORD? Will you forget me forever?

Or this one from Psalm 10:
Why, LORD, do you stand far off?
Why do you hide yourself in times of trouble?

Or this one from Psalm 43:
Why have you rejected me?

Or this one from Psalm 83 about enemies:
Make them like tumbleweed. . . .
Terrify them with your storm.
Cover their faces with shame. . . .
May they perish in disgrace.

Anger, hurt, isolation, vengeance, rage, betrayal—it's all there in the Psalms. There is a lot of
God is good
in the Psalms,
and there's a ton of
Where the hell are you?

The question is:
Why have these poems and prayers endured?
Why, thousands of years later, do we still have them?

And the answer you'll return to again and again is:
They speak to our human experience.

We relate.
We know what the writer is talking about.
Especially the vicious stuff. The lines where the writer wants God to destroy their enemy. Who hasn't felt that before?

The Psalms show us what healthy spiritual life looks like. You name everything that's happening inside of you. You give it language and expression. You articulate exactly what the desolation feels like.

If you don't drag it up and give it words, then it's buried down in your being somewhere. And it will come out in other ways. Unhealthy, destructive ways. You'll keep it all bottled up. And you'll be miserable.

These prayers and poems in the Psalms have endured because they speak something true about our hearts and minds and hopes and feelings and desires and wounds. That's the power of the Psalms. That's the power of the Bible.

Or the prophets.
Toward the end of the Hebrew scriptures are the books about the prophets, from Jeremiah and Isaiah to Nahum and the shepherd Amos.

They're a strange group,

ranting and raving about the corruption of the religious and
economic and government systems,
insisting that God hates the religious festivals—
literally,

Isaiah has God saying,
I cannot bear your worthless assemblies. . . .
I hate with all my being. . . .
I hide my eyes from you;
even when you offer many prayers.

Amos announces God's anger at the injustice with
Hear this, you who trample the needy . . .

Micah calls out those who
covet fields and seize them,
and houses, and take them.

While Habakkuk cries,
Woe to him who piles up stolen goods
and makes himself wealthy by extortion!

Why have the writings of the prophets endured?
Because they fearlessly speak truth to power.
They call out the injustice and oppression of the system
gone wrong.
They hold those in leadership accountable for the decisions
they make.

Some have argued that in the prophets, we have the first
articulations in human history of a coherent vision for social
justice. So every time you listen to a Rage Against the Machine
song or hear a politician pointing out how the system works for
some while it leaves others out in the cold or see a documentary

that exposes some fraud or greed, you're seeing the spirit of the prophets alive and well.

Or the parable of the prodigal son,
which should probably be called the parable of the forgiving father.
Jesus told this story about a—
wait, you've read it, right?
It's incredible. In just a few words, we get this gut-wrenching
story of two sons who are both separated from their father—one
because of his bad deeds, one because of his good deeds.

And both are welcomed home.
The one has left and realized what he's missing.
The other hasn't left and doesn't seem to understand what he's
had all along.

And both are loved and invited to come home.
It's a story about exile,
about all of the ways we wander from the love that's been ours the
whole time,
looking for our worth and value in all sorts of things and people
when we've been a child of a loving father the whole time.

Home, according to the story,
is both a geographical location
and a state of being.

And then there's the story about Jacob in the book of Genesis.
After we meet him, he says,
I am Esau,
because he's pretending to be his brother.
And then later, toward the end of his story, he wrestles by a river
and when he's asked his name he says,
Jacob.

This is a story about a man becoming comfortable in his own skin, owning up to his true self. He's no longer pretending to be someone else—he's ready to step into his destiny. And when he finally says that he's Jacob, he's told that his name is going to be changed!

Or Daniel—
who's stripped of his name and family and customs and taken to a foreign land where he's indoctrinated into the life of the Babylonians. Everything known and familiar is taken from him, and yet he maintains his sense of self and his integrity.

And then there's Mother Mary.
She's told that God has big plans for her, plans that will come with a cost. She ponders these things
in her heart.
And then in the end, when her boy is killed, she's there.

There's a heart and soul to these stories, a raw and vulnerable humanity shimmering through these accounts of people wrestling with death and identity and injustice and forgiveness and love.

————————

And so you keep reading these stories, asking why people wrote them down in the first place and then asking why they've endured.

What do they say about what it means to be human?
What do they teach us about hope and love and pain and loss and forgiveness and betrayal and compassion?
How do these stories help us better understand our stories?

Often, especially when people come to a particularly strange or gruesome or inexplicable passage, they'll ask,
Why did God say this?

The better question is:
Why did people find it important to tell this story?

Followed by:
What was it that moved them to record these words?

Followed by:
What was happening in the world at that time?

And then:
What does this passage/story/poem/verse/book tell us about how people understood who they were and who God was at that time?

And then:
What's the story that's unfolding here, and why did these people think it was a story worth telling?

Part 5

Endnotes

A Note About the Subtitle

The line about *the way you think and feel about everything* is a respectful nod to Thomas Cahill's brilliant book *The Gifts of the Jews,* which is subtitled *How a Tribe of Desert Nomads Changed the Way Everyone Thinks and Feels.*

A Disclaimer About This Book

There's a ton I left out.

If you finished this book and your first thought was *But he left out the passage from the book of _____ that deals with _____,*

you're right, I did.
I left it out.
And there's a very specific reason I left it out: if I didn't, then this book would be called

the *Bible*.

A Thousand Thanks

Thanks to

Stratton Glaze for being the Rick Rubin of this book.

Chris Ferebee for being a great friend and agent for sixteen years.

Jeremy Smoak—you can run but you can't hide.

Mark Bass for the cover art.

And all the good people at HarperOne, from Mickey Maudlin to Mark Tauber, Laina Adler, Suzanne Wickham, Lisa Zuniga, Anna Paustenbauch, and Anne Edwards.

Books About the Bible That Will Blow Your Mind

If you were reading this book and continually said to yourself, *I haven't heard any of this. Where did he find this?* there are lots of answers to that question. So here you are, a reading list to get you started:

First,
I'd recommend starting with two books by Thomas Cahill:
The Gifts of the Jews: How a Tribe of Desert Nomads Changed the Way Everyone Thinks and Feels
and then
Desire of the Everlasting Hills: The World Before and After Jesus.

If you're interested in the history and background of the Hebrew scriptures, try Bruce Feiler's books:
Walking the Bible: A Journey by Land Through the Five Books of Moses
and
Where God Was Born: A Daring Adventure Through the Bible's Greatest Stories.
(He includes in the back of each of them an extensive list of references. Pure gold there.)

As far as commentaries on the Hebrew scriptures, here's a
great one:
The Five Books of Miriam: A Woman's Commentary on the Torah
by Ellen Frankel.
And then there's
The JPS Torah Commentary series
and
The Bible As It Was by James L. Kugel (which is amazing).

How to Read the Bible

Now, a few about Jesus.
If you're new to the idea that Jesus was Jewish and everything he
does is in that context, I'd start with the following:
*Understanding the Difficult Words of Jesus: New Insights from a
Hebraic Perspective* by David Bivin and Roy Blizzard Jr.
then
*Poet and Peasant: A Literary-Cultural Approach to the Parables in
Luke* by Kenneth E. Bailey
then
Our Father Abraham: Jewish Roots of the Christian Faith by
Marvin R. Wilson
then
Excavating Jesus: Beneath the Stones, Behind the Texts by John
Dominic Crossan and Jonathan L. Reed.

New to the first-century political and economic background of the
Christmas story?
Read
The Liberation of Christmas: The Infancy Narratives in Social Context
by Richard A. Horsley.
May I introduce you to a man named N. T. Wright? Get a book
of his with *Jesus* in the title, sit down in a comfortable chair, and
prepare to be fire-hosed. I'd also recommend his New Testament
for Everyone series:
[Name of Bible book] for Everyone. Like *Luke for Everyone, Mark for
Everyone*, etc.

Add to the list any book by John Dominic Crossan. I'd start with
God and Empire: Jesus Against Rome, Then and Now.
And then of course there's Abraham Joshua Heschel. Try these
books:
The Prophets
or
God in Search of Man: A Philosophy of Judaism
or
Moral Grandeur and Spiritual Audacity.

Good books on the book of Revelation?
Christ and the Caesars by Ethelbert Stauffer (how great is his name?)
and
Reversed Thunder: The Revelation of John and the Praying Imagination
by Eugene H. Peterson.

Want to read the Gospels in a whole new way?
Read these:
Heart and Mind: The Four-Gospel Journey for Radical Transformation
by Alexander John Shaia,
God, the Bible, and Human Consciousness by Nancy Tenfelde Clasby
(so good), and
God Was in This Place and I, I Did Not Know by Lawrence Kushner.
(Kushner's book is an excellent example of what it looks like to turn
the gem. In this case, each chapter of Kushner's book is an entirely
different interpretation of one story in the Bible.)
I highly recommend Kenton L. Sparks's outstanding book,
*Sacred Word, Broken Word: Biblical Authority and the Dark Side of
Scripture,*
and
*The Bible Tells Me So . . . : Why Defending Scripture Has Made Us
Unable to Read It* by Peter Enns.
One of my favorite writers is Robert Farrar Capon. Start with
The Mystery of Christ . . . and Why We Don't Get It.

Then go to
The Parables of Grace.
Chapter 3 of Dallas Willard's book
The Divine Conspiracy: Rediscovering Our Hidden Life in God
changed everything for me.

Jürgen Moltmann wrote a book called
The Spirit of Life: A Universal Affirmation.
I'm still recovering.

A Note on Growing and Changing

A question I often get asked: *What do I do if I'm growing and changing and my spiritual perspectives are expanding but my family and friends aren't seeing what I'm seeing?*

You can't take people where they don't want to go. The thing that you are so happy to be freed from still works for some people. They like it. It feels safe. It provides meaning and security. So when you challenge it and quote whoever you've been reading lately and ask the questions that opened new doors for you, they do not find this energizing.

Groups have a center of gravity. Families, friends, churches, offices, and schools all have a dominant consciousness, a center of gravity, a party line. It's the often unspoken agreement that keeps things running smoothly based on what to believe, how to behave, what's acceptable, and what isn't. So when you charge in all excited about whatever it is you've learned, you are a disruption. And systems don't take kindly to disruptions, often expending extraordinary energy to quell the disruption, pushing it to the edges, discrediting it. This is why some churches ban books, this is why certain topics are off-limits at family gatherings, and this is often why people use words like *heretic*.

Because of this, some voices that you once listened to will no longer be helpful. In fact, some voices that once *helped* you, if you continue to listen to them, will *hinder* your growth.

It may even feel like a step backward—because it is.

This is normal. Painful, but normal. If you continue to listen to them as you get increasingly frustrated and angry, it is not their fault—it is yours. They are continuing to do and be who they have always been; it is you who has changed. It is your responsibility to stop listening to voices that hinder your ongoing growth and maturity.

You may need to create boundaries with certain people. For some people, it will appear as though you are going off the deep end, and they may see it as their sacred task to rescue you. No matter how earnest they are, their constant desire to engage you may not be very life-giving, and you may have to kindly but firmly say to them, *We are not going to have this conversation again.*

Also, you may be kind and gracious and generous, and you still may lose friends. You may be labeled something crazy and untrue. You may find that certain people avoid you. This can be disorienting, to say the least. In those moments, when you are feeling the cold, stiff breeze of loneliness, ask yourself this question: *Would I rather go back?*

Would you rather be alive and free and open and thrilled with all that is happening in your heart, or would you rather go back to who and how you were before? I didn't think so. Remember that.

It is very difficult to find words for experiences. You may be exploding with new insights and hope and life, but if your friends haven't experienced something similar, you going on and on and on about it may not be helping them see what you've seen. In fact, it may be causing harm. Be patient. Don't force your experiences on others. The moving of spirit is a great mystery, and how or why or when certain people wake up is beyond us. Let people have their own experiences.

Bitterness is not your friend. It's easy to become cynical, focusing your energies on *them* and endlessly wondering why *they* aren't more evolved and why *they* are still stuck back there, repeating the same slogans and going through the same motions. If you are filled with pride over how free and intelligent and enlightened you are in comparison to their backward, antiquated ways, your new knowledge has simply made you arrogant. Watch your heart carefully, because if you aren't more compassionate and more kind and more understanding, then you haven't grown at all.

Celebrate. Think back over the last six months, over the last year, over the last five years. You aren't the person you were. You've grown, evolved, opened up, been set free. Celebrate that. Not because you're so great, but because you're grateful. If all of the new things you've experienced don't first and foremost make you grateful, then what have you gained?

For Jesus the point is fruit. You'll know people by their fruit, by their life, by how they actually live in the world. Lots of people get excited about new ideas, and then they shove these new understandings in other people's faces and become the very thing they despise. (If you have bought more than five copies of *Love Wins* for the same person and they still haven't read it, I'm talking about you. Ha-ha.) If a new idea or understanding or interpretation doesn't help transform you into the kind of person Jesus is calling us all to be, then it isn't worth much. Are you more forgiving than you were? Less judgmental? More present? More courageous?

Less worried and anxious, more free and loving? That's what's interesting, you being transformed.

Remember that you are not alone. Never, ever forget this. Especially if you've begun to despair that you're the only one who sees it like this. You're not alone.